Diabetic Air Fryer Cookbook

365 Quick and Easy Low Fat, Low Sugar, and Low Carb Air fryer Recipes for a Healthy Life

-By Olivia Kaur

Copyright © [2022] Olivia Kaur
All rights reserved

All rights to the book displayed here are solely owned by the author. It is against the law to use or copy the content, and if you want to, you need to get the author's permission.

Table of contents

Introductions 6

PART I: 8

DIABETES AND OBESITY 8

PART II: 12

HEALTHY LIVING AND AIR-FRYING 12

CHAPTER III: 16

DIABETIC DIETARY REQUIREMENTS 16

BREAKFAST RECIPES 21

    air fried Eggs 21
    Pancakes with Cinnamon 22
    Scrambled eggs 22
    Frittata with fennel 23
    Oatmeal with strawberries 23
    Frittata with mushrooms and cheese 24
    Pancakes with Cinnamon and Cheese 24
    Eggs Hard-Boiled 25
    Frittata with White Eggs and Spinach 25
    Sandwich with Scallions 26
    Bacon in the Air Fryer 26
    Sandwiches with grilled cheese 27
    Omelet with asparagus 27
    Omelet Oriental 28
    Crispy Avocado Fries for Breakfast 28
    Frittata for breakfast 29
    Breakfast Mini Cheeseburger Sliders 29
    Rolls with bacon and cheese 30

APPETIZER AND SIDES RECIPES 31

    Chips with garlic and kale 31
    Balls of salmon and garlic 31
    Onions rings 32
    Fries with Crispy Eggplant 33
    Bell Peppers Charred 33
    Stew with mushrooms 34
    Cheese and onion nuggets 35
    Nuts with Spices 35
    French fries made with ketones 36
    Green Garlic Tomatoes Fried 36
    Tots with Garlic and Cauliflower 37

POULTRY RECIPES 38

Salad with warm chicken and spinach	38
Crispy Chicken Wings in a Pair	39
The Whole Italian Chicken	40
Pot Pie with Chicken	41
Chicken Casserole	42
Macaroni and Cheese with Chicken	43
Casserole with Broccoli and Chicken	44
Tikka Chicken Kebabs	45
Chicken and Bacon Wrapped	46
Thighs of creamy chicken	47
Teriyaki Hen Drumsticks in the Air Fryer	48

BEEF RECIPES **49**

Wraps filled with meatloaf	49
A burger with two cheeses	50
Schnitzel (beef)	50
Bundles of steak with asparagus	51
Hamburgers	52
Kabobs of Beef Steak with Vegetables	53
Steak Rib-Eye	54
Sloppy Joes without meat	54
"Curry with Beef"	55
Salad with Asian Grilled Beef	56
Pot Roast on Sunday	57
Fajita Bowls with Beef and Peppers	58

PORK RECIPES **60**

Pork Ribs in Country Style	60
Dijon Tenderloin de Pork	61
Satay Pork	62
Air Fryer Pork Taquitos	63
Delectable Egg Rolls	63
Dumplings with Pork	64
Broccoli with Pork Chops	65
Chops de pork avec sauce cheesy	66
Nachos with Pork Rind	66

FISH & SEAFOOD RECIPES **68**

Air Fryer Salmon Cakes	68
Shrimp in Coconut Sauce	68
Air Fryer Crispy Fish Sticks	69
Salmon with Honey Glaze	70
Salmon with basil-parmesan crust	71
Cajun Shrimp in the Air Fryer	72
Lemon Cod in the Air Fryer	72
Salmon Fillets in the Air Fryer	73
Fish and Chips in the Air Fryer	73
Grilled Lemon-Glazed Salmon	74
Nuggets of air-fried fish	75

    Grilled Garlic Rosemary Prawns 76

VEGETARIAN RECIPES 77
    Surprise Eggplant.. 77
    Turnips with carrots 78
    In an Instant, Brussels Sprouts with Parmesan 78
    Fennel Braised.. 79
    Salad with beets and oranges 80
    A Dish with Endives 81
    Roasted potatoes 82
    Mushrooms stuffed with cheese 82
    Skewers with Mediterranean vegetables 83

SNACKS RECIPES 84
    fried sweet potatoes 84
    Cheese skewers 85
    Zoodles Crisps 85
    Pumpkin Skinny Chips... 86
    Ripe bananas fried in the air. 87
    Air-fried plantains with coconut sauce 87
    Bruschetta with basil pesto 88
    Apple Cinnamon Chips 89
    Triangles of Phyllo vegetables 89

DESSERTS RECIPES 91
    Tapioca Pudding is delicious 91
    Bread Pudding with Vanilla 92
    Blueberry Muffins.. 93
    Mini Chocolate Cake 94
    Flavorful Carrot Halva. 95
    Vermicelli Pudding 95
    Custard with Yogurt 96

CONCLUSION 98

INTRODUCTIONS

Obesity is a medical condition in which a person has acquired too much body fat, which may have a negative impact on their health. This differs from getting overweight, which is caused by increased bone, muscle mass, fat, or bodily water. Obesity is defined as weighing at least 20 pounds more than a healthy weight. Obesity may arise due to a variety of factors, including overeating, an inactive lifestyle, and insufficient sleep. Obesity, regardless of the reason, raises the risk of major ailments such as heart disease, type 2 diabetes, and high blood pressure.

Obese people are more likely to develop type 2 diabetes, which is also known as adult-onset diabetes or insulin resistance. This is a condition in which the level of glucose in the blood is constantly high. Fat tissue cells in obese persons may metabolise more calories than they can ingest. Inflammation causes cytokinesis, which is generated by the strain in these cells caused by eating too many nutrients. As a result, cytokines block insulin receptor signals, enabling cells to gradually develop immune to insulin. Insulin promotes cells to utilise glucose for nourishment. Because your cells are immune to insulin, your body will be unable to convert the glucose into energy, resulting in a constantly increased blood glucose level.

Stress often causes cell inflammation and may lead to heart failure, as well as lowering normal insulin responses. Obesity or overweight increases the likelihood of developing type 2 diabetes; the body retains ample insulin, but the cells have grown resistant to insulin's activity. Extra weight puts pressure on the insides of human cells. When there are more nutrients to absorb than the cells can accept, the cell's membrane sends a warning signal instructing the cell to reduce the insulin cell surface receptors. One of the prominent diabetes signs is insulin resistance and consistently increased blood sugar glucose levels.

Diabetes patients are more prone than non-diabetics to suffer significant cardiac issues such as diabetic cardiomyopathy, coronary artery disease, and heart failure. Because of the development of fatty substances in the arteries, the heart must work extra hard in obese or diabetic persons to move blood throughout the body. Weight loss is an essential strategy for persons suffering from obesity, especially those with type 2 diabetes. Moderate and regular weight loss, of at least 510 percent, will boost insulin activity, lower fasting blood glucose levels, and lessen the requirement for some diabetic medications.

You must change your lifestyle to cure diabetes symptoms or, at the very least, lower your risk of developing diabetes. An exercise, healthy food, and behaviour modification programme that will successfully treat obesity. These factors will greatly help you manage obesity and type 2 diabetes.

- Dietary balance and health
- Exercise and medications

Physical activity is as important as medicine, but an air fryer may help with a healthy and balanced diet.

You may lose weight by controlling your diet and paying attention to what you eat and how it affects your body. Healthy fried dishes are increasingly available. Although fried foods are associated with health, it is now feasible to prepare healthy foods using an air fryer. Air frying is, by some measures, easier than cooking in oil. It cuts calories by 70–80% and has a lot less fat.

This method of cooking may help reduce the negative effects of oil frying. When you fry starchy meals, the chemical acrylamide is formed, which has been linked to an increased risk of cancer. Air fryers provide the taste, texture, and golden-brown colour of oil-fried dishes without the calories. Air fryers are cooking appliances that cook food by spinning warm air over it. Air-fried meals are said to be safer and healthier than deep-fried dishes since they use less oil to create a similar taste and texture.

You may now eat a healthier kind of fast food without fear of the repercussions.

PART I:

DIABETES AND OBESITY

SEVEN ESSENTIAL DIABETES PREVENTIVE ACTIONS

- I became more active
- Consume fiber-rich foods.
- Consume whole grains.
- Slim down
- Make healthier decisions.
- I do not smoke.
- Consume in moderation.

Diabetes is a difficult disease that occurs for two reasons: when the pancreas does not create enough insulin to meet the body's demands, or when the insulin produced is not adequately used by the body. Insulin is a hormone that regulates blood sugar levels. Hyperglycemia, or high blood sugar, is a common complication of untreated diabetes, causing long-term damage to the body's components, particularly blood vessels and neurons. Diabetes mellitus is a group of diseases that affect how the body uses glucose. Glucose is necessary for your health. The cells that make up muscles and tissues need a large amount of glucose. It also serves as the brain's principal power source. The fundamental problem with diabetes differs depending on the kind of diabetes. And, regardless of the kind of diabetes, this may result in an excess of sugar in the blood. Excess sugar consumption may result in serious health problems. The insulin hormone transports sugar from the blood into the cells.

High blood sugar levels may affect your kidneys, eyes, organs, and nerves.

To understand the main cause of diabetes, you must first understand how the body usually takes in glucose.

HOW GLUCOSE AND INSULIN INTERACT

- Insulin is produced by the pancreas, which is located behind and below the stomach. It is a hormone that controls the amount of sugar in the blood. Here is a step-by-step look at how insulin is made in the body. Insulin is made by the pancreas.

- The sugar is then helped into the bodily cells by insulin.
- Insulin lowers the amount of sugar in the blood.
- Because the blood sugar level has dropped, the pancreas has secreted less insulin.
- As blood sugar levels fall in the body, insulin release from the pancreas decreases.

DIABETES TYPES

Diabetes mellitus, generally known as diabetes, is a metabolic condition that causes increased blood sugar levels. The hormone insulin transports sugar from the blood into cells to be digested or utilised for nourishment. Diabetes occurs when the body does not produce enough insulin or does not use the insulin produced effectively. Diabetes-related uncontrolled increases in blood sugar levels may harm your brain, lungs, kidneys, and other organs.

Diabetes is classified into many types:

Type 1 diabetes

Type 1 diabetes, commonly known as insulin-dependent diabetes or juvenile diabetes, is caused by an immune system deficit or an autoimmune illness. Your immune system attacks insulin-producing cells in the pancreas, thereby eliminating the body's ability to produce insulin. It is unclear what causes autoimmune illness or how to properly treat it. You must take insulin to live with Type 1 diabetes. Several people are diagnosed as infants or young adults. Type 1 diabetes affects just 10% of patients with diabetes. Polyuria (excessive excretion of urine), polydipsia (severe thirst), abrupt weight loss, continuous hunger, weariness, and visual abnormalities are symptoms of type 1 diabetes. These shifts might happen quickly.

Diabetes Type 2

It is caused by the body's insufficient insulin utilisation and is also known as adult-onset diabetes or non-insulin-dependent diabetes. The majority of people with diabetes have type 2 diabetes. The symptoms may be similar to those of type 1 diabetes. However, when symptoms have already developed, the problem might be recognised after several years of diagnosis, which is considerably less noticeable.

Type 2 diabetes develops when sugar levels in the blood rise and the body develops insulin resistance. Insulin resistance is the cause of type 2 diabetes.

This eventually leads to obesity. This is a list of several illnesses on its own. Older generations were more vulnerable, but younger generations are feeling the effects more acutely. This is the result of poor health, insufficient nutrition, and poor exercise habits. In type 2 diabetes, your pancreas prevents insulin from being adequately used. This is problematic because sugar must be removed from circulation and stored in cells for energy.

Finally, this will increase the demand for insulin therapy. Earlier phases, such as prediabetes, may be effectively managed with diet, exercise, and dynamic blood sugar management. This will also prevent the growth of type 2 diabetes. Diabetes may be kept track of. In certain cases, if adequate dietary changes are made, the body will go into remission.

Diabetes During Pregnancy

Gestational diabetes is defined as hyperglycemia (blood glucose levels above average but below diabetes levels). Prenatal tests are used to detect gestational diabetes rather than indications such as elevated blood sugar, which also happens throughout pregnancy. Insulin-blocking hormones released by the placenta are the primary cause of this kind of diabetes. Food and exercise may help you control gestational diabetes most of the time. It is usually rectified after delivery. Gestational diabetes increases the risk of problems during pregnancy. It will also increase the chances of both moms and babies developing type 2 diabetes later in life. The synthesis of insulin-blocking substances by the placenta causes this kind of diabetes.

DIABETES'S ROOT CAUSES

Type 1 diabetes causes

The cause of type 1 diabetes is unknown. The immune system is thought to target and eliminate insulin-producing cells (in the pancreas). Viruses and infectious germs are often destroyed by the immune system. This leaves the human body with little or no insulin. Instead of being transported into cells, sugar accumulates in the circulation.

Type 1 diabetes is thought to be caused by a combination of inherited vulnerability and environmental factors, although the exact nature of those factors is unknown. Weight is not thought to be a variable in type 1 diabetes. Type 1 occurs when the beta cells that create insulin in the pancreas are targeted and destroyed by the body's immune system, which is the body's capacity to battle illness. Scientists believe that type 1 diabetes is caused by hereditary factors as well as environmental factors.

Prediabetes and Type 2 Diabetes Causes

In prediabetes, your cells may stop responding to insulin, which can also happen in type 2 diabetes, and your pancreas can't make enough insulin to make up for this. Sugar begins to accumulate in your circulation rather than travel to your cells, where it is needed for fuel. Although genetic and environmental variables are thought to have a role in type 2 diabetes development, it is unknown why this happens.

Obesity is linked to the progression of type 2 diabetes, albeit not everyone with type 2 is fat. The most common kind of diabetes is caused by a combination of factors, including eating habits and genetic make-up.

Here are a few examples:

- ✓ **Insulin sensitivity**

Insulin resistance, a disorder in which the body, liver, and fat cells cannot handle insulin properly, is a frequent progression of type 2 diabetes. As a result, the body needs more insulin to allow glucose to reach cells. To meet the increased demand, the pancreas produces more insulin at first. Over time, the pancreas can't make enough insulin, so glucose levels in the blood rise.

- ✓ **Obesity, obesity, and being overweight**

You are significantly more likely to develop type 2 diabetes if you are not consistently participating and are fat or overweight. Excess weight often causes insulin resistance, which is more prevalent in those with type 2 diabetes. In which the body's fat deposits play an important role Excess abdominal fat is linked to insulin resistance, type 2 diabetes, heart and blood vessel problems.

- ✓ **Genes and family trees**

A family history of diabetes increases the likelihood of gestational diabetes in a woman, suggesting that genes play a role. Changes in the genes of African Americans, Asians, American Indians, Latinas, and Hispanics could also be a reason why the illness is becoming more common.

Any gene may make you more prone to developing type 2 diabetes or type 1 diabetes.

Obesity may be exacerbated by genetic factors, leading to type 2 diabetes.

PART II:

HEALTHY LIVING AND AIR-FRYING

In terms of roasting and baking, an air fryer is similar to an oven. Still, the heating components are only on top and are assisted by a powerful, huge fan, resulting in beautifully crisp food in no time. Instead of a vat of boiling oil, the air fryer uses rotating heated air to conveniently and consistently cook food. This is placed in a metal basket (mesh) or a rack to enable hot air to circulate uniformly over the food, providing the same light golden, crispy crunch as frying in oil. It's a simple air fryer that cooks food quicker than frying and cleans up easily. You may make a variety of nutritious meals such as fruits, meat, fish, chicken, and more, as well as healthier versions of your favourite fried dishes such as chips, onion rings, or French fries.

How Does an Air Fryer Work?

The air fryer is a convection oven with a hotter countertop. Its small size allows for much faster cooking. A heating device and a fan are kept at the top of the device. Hot air circulates through and around the food in a basket-style fryer. This rapid circulation, like deep frying, crisps the food. It's also quite easy to clean, and most systems include dishwasher-safe components.

Using an Air Fryer to Cook?

Once you understand how to operate an air fryer, you may use it to heat frozen items or cook fresh dishes such as chicken, salmon, other shellfish, pork chops, and veggies. Most meats do not need extra oil since they are still moist.

- Season well with salt and your preferred herbs and spices.
- Use dry spices; less moisture results in crisper results.
- Wait until the final few minutes of cooking to best the steak with any sauce or barbecue sauce.
- Browning is required for lean meat cuts or things with little or no fat, while crisping requires a spray of oil. Before cooking, clean the pork chops and boneless chicken breasts and lightly oil them. Vegetable oil or canola oil is often used because it has a higher smoke point and can stand up to the high heat of an air fryer.
- Vegetables are often coated with oil before being air-fried.

- Season them with salt. Use less than you normally would.
- The crunchy parts that are air-fried provide a lot of taste. Baby potato halves, broccoli florets, and Brussels sprouts are all delicious when fried. They're so clean. Sweet potatoes, butternut squash, peppers, and green beans all tend to get sweeter as they cook.

For Beginners: Air Fryer Cooking Tips

✓ **Shake the container:**

Open the fryer and move the food about as it cooks on the device's tray, compressing smaller meals like French fries and chips. To improve performance, toss them every 510 minutes.

✓ **Avoid overcrowding the basket:**

Giving food enough space so that air can flow properly is what results in crispy results.

✓ **Spray the food with oil:**

Check that the food does not stick to the bowl. Brush meals lightly with cooking spray.

✓ **Keep your meal dry:**

Before frying, ensure the food is completely dry to avoid splattering and excessive smoke (even if you marinate it). Similarly, while producing high-fat dishes like chicken wings, be sure to frequently clean the oil from the bottom of the machine.

✓ **Other uses for air frying include:**

The air fryer is great for grilling, baking, and roasting, all of which are healthy ways to cook.

✓ **Other suggestions include**
- To ensure even cooking, divide the meal into equal portions. Distribute the food in the air fryer basket in a single thin, uniform layer. Food may get less crispy if the basket is overcrowded.
- A little bit of oil would provide the same light, golden, crispy crust as frying. Use cooking spray or an oil mister to put a thin, even layer of oil on the food.
- The air fryer is useful for reheating dishes, especially those with a crispy exterior.

The Advantages of Using an Air Fryer

- easy to clean
- Low-fat foods
- Less oil is required.

- Hot air evenly cooks food.
- Loss of weight
- Cancer risk is reduced.
- Diabetes administration
- Memory enhancement
- Better gut health

This food pyramid recommends consuming a significant quantity of nutritious vegetables and whole-grain starches, a balanced amount of healthy fats and proteins, and a small amount of nuts and oils.

HEALTHY HABITS OF LIVING AND EATING

To get maximum health advantages, the appropriate mix of several nutrients is required. In general, a healthy diet includes the following food groups:

- Reduce your intake of starchy foods, including potatoes, bread, pasta, and rice.
- Vegetables and fruits in plenty.
- Dairy and milk items in small quantities.
- Meat, fish, and eggs are examples of protein foods.
- Nondairy protein sources include beans, almonds, lentils, and tofu.
- Fatty and sugary foods are the fifth food group you eat. However, sugary and fatty foods may make up just a small portion of the diet.
- a little part of what you eat
- Salmon, sardines, and pilchards must be consumed.
- Dark green vegetables, such as broccoli and kale, must be consumed.
- Calcium-rich foods include fruit juices and soy products.
- Fortified cereals and fatty fish are good sources of vitamin D. It helps the body assimilate calcium, so aim to get enough vitamin D from the sun and include vitamin D-containing foods in your diet.
- Replace saturated fat with polyunsaturated fat as required.
- Consume at least five servings of vegetables and fruits every day.
- At least two pieces of fish every week (ideally fatty fish).
- Begin eating whole grains and nuts on a regular basis.
- Limit your salt intake to no more than 6 g each day.
- Alcohol consumption has been restricted.

Dietary Limits or Avoidance of the Following

- Meats that have been commercially created or processed, or ready-made meals that are rich in trans fatty acids and salt
- Grain products that have been refined, such as dry cereals or white bread,
- Sugary drinks with added sugar.
- Cookies, sweets, and crisps are examples of high-calorie yet nutritionally deficient foods.

All of the Following Constitute a Well-Balanced Diet

- To be productive throughout the day, you must have stamina.
- The nutrients you need for growth and repair help you stay healthy and balanced and keep you from getting diseases like diabetes and some cancers that are linked to diet.
- You might also be able to keep a healthier weight if you stay active and eat a healthy, well-balanced diet.
- Some important nutrients, like vitamins C, A, B, and E, selenium, zinc, and iron, could hurt parts of the immune system.
- By keeping a healthy weight and eating a diet low in saturated fat and high in fibre from whole grains, you can lower your chances of getting type 2 diabetes, improve your heart health, and strengthen your teeth and bones.
- Eating a well-balanced diet and getting enough exercise can also help you lose weight, decrease your cholesterol and blood pressure, and lessen your risk of developing type 2 diabetes.

Your Blood Glucose Level Should Look Like This

MG/DL	FASTING	AFTER EATING	TWO-THREE AFTER EATING
NORMAL	80-100	170-200	120-140
GLUCOSE DEFICIENCY	101-125	190-230	140-160
DIABETIC	126+	220-300	200+

CHAPTER III:

DIABETIC DIETARY REQUIREMENTS

Nutrition is an important factor to consider while managing diabetes. A well-balanced diet can help you regulate and maintain your blood sugar levels, among other things. You should find a good balance between what you drink and what you eat to keep your blood sugar level stable.

What you eat, how much you eat, and when you eat are all important factors in controlling your blood sugar levels. The solution to all of this will be shared with you here.

MACRONUTRIENTS

We can't speak about healthy living without considering macronutrients. So, what exactly are they?

Macronutrients are also known as macronutrients. They are nutrients that our bodies need in great amounts in order to operate effectively. The nutrients provide your body energy in the form of kilocalories or calories. Macronutrients are classified into three categories:

CARBOHYDRATES

Carbohydrates fuel the body. They degrade into glucose and monosaccharaides. Carbohydrates are not all created equal; they might be simple or complicated.

Simple carbs:

These are made up of tiny molecules that are quickly digested and cause a fast spike in glucose levels. Unlike simple carbohydrates, bigger molecules are broken down into smaller molecules in complex carbohydrates. They are slow to digest and raise blood sugar levels.

Rapid carbohydrate ingestion raises plasma glucose levels, which is evaluated by a glycemic index. Consuming carbohydrates with a high glycemic index may quickly raise your blood glucose levels. On the other hand, if you eat meals with a low glycemic load, your blood glucose level will slowly rise over time.

PROTEIN

Protein provides amino acids to the body; amino acids are used in the activities of the brain, blood, nervous system, hair, and skin. It is also responsible for transporting oxygen and other critical nutrients throughout the body. When carbs and glucose are unavailable, the body wills reverse-process protein in order to get energy.

Your body can produce 11 amino acids on its own and get the other nine from nutrition.

There are two kinds of protein: animal protein and plant protein. Plant-based proteins include seeds, nuts, and cereals. Meat, fish, eggs, and dairy products are the most prevalent sources of protein.

According to the USDA, protein sources should account for between 10% and 30% of your daily calorie needs.

FATS

People generally see fat as harmful and attempt to avoid it in their diet. However, dietary fat is essential in your quest to keep your blood sugar levels low. Good fats preserve your organs, enable optimal cell activity, and are essential for insulin production. In the case of calorie restriction or starvation, fat may provide energy.

While good fats are essential for a balanced diet, poor fats may lead to obesity over time. Fats should be ingested in moderation to maintain a healthy weight. Let's take a short look at the various forms of fat.

Saturated fatty acids:

Saturated fats are found in dairy products and beef. They are solid at room temperature and may be shelf-stable for some time. Unsaturated fats: These are either monounsaturated or polyunsaturated fats. They are derived from meat and certain plant sources and are quite helpful. They are liquid at room temperature and will stay so after refrigeration. They are less stable than saturated fats.

Trans Fatty Acids:

These are polyunsaturated fats that transform from liquid to solid form and are severely harmful to your health. They are found in processed foods, fast foods, cakes, cookies, and other foods containing hydrogenated fats.

OTHER VITAL NUTRIENTS

Aside from macronutrients, which supply nutrition to your body, there are additional critical nutrients to consider. These nutrients are also necessary and should be included in your diet.

D VITAMIN

Vitamin D is a little-considered fat-soluble hormone with several advantages. It aids in the maintenance of joints, bones, and teeth, as well as the immune system. Nuts, eggs, seeds, butter, and fatty fish are examples of foods that contain the vitamin.

Also, if you go out in the sun for 30 minutes every day, you make more vitamin D and lower your risk of getting diabetes.

MAGNESIUM

This is an essential vitamin in your diet. According to research, patients with type 2 diabetes are more likely to have a magnesium shortage. Intracellular magnesium is in charge of vascular tone, insulin action, and insulin-mediated glucose absorption. So, being magnesium deficient is bad since it may aggravate insulin resistance. Correcting a magnesium deficit can substantially improve your ability to manage your disease.

SODIUM

Sodium's purpose in the body is to convey nerve impulses and to regulate the electric charge both within and outside your cells. We are more likely to ingest salt than we desire when we eat largely processed meals. While high salt consumption is unhealthy, a low sodium intake may cause insulin resistance and cause cardiovascular disease.

A daily consumption of 2,300 milligrams should not be exceeded, according to the American Dietary Guidelines. If possible, keep it around 1,500 mg; the less, the better.

DIABETES NUTRIENT RECOMMENDATIONS

When managing diabetes, nutrition is an important factor that must be considered. What enters your system contributes to your overall health.

Glucose level in the blood To keep your blood sugar levels stable, you must watch what you consume. As a result, I'll be discussing the suggested diabetic nutrients with you. These are some nutritious things to have on hand in your kitchen.

VEGETABLES

- Carrots

- Broccoli
- Tomatoes
- Peas in a green colour
- "Green chilli pepper"

FRUITS

- Fruits (strawberries, blueberries, blackberries)
- Oranges
- Citrus
- Apples
- Grapes

WHOLE GRAINS (GRAINS)

- Oats
- Quinoa
- Barley
- Cornmeal
- Brown rice
- Low-fat dairy
- Yogurt
- Milk
- Cheese
- Soy milk, almond milk

PROTEIN

- Skinless turkey or chicken
- Meat that is lean
- Eggs
- Fish
- Nuts
- split peas
- Chickpeas
- Dried legumes
- Meat alternatives (tofu)

You are not confined to the foods I have suggested above. You may consume other healthy meals as well. When cooking, use oils instead of stick margarine, shortening, and lard. Also, incorporate meals high in heart-healthy fats into your diet. Avocado, olive oil, canola oil, nuts and seeds, tuna, salmon, and mackerel are just a few examples.

Each vitamin has a distinct purpose in the body. Because you are managing a health issue, you must balance them to prevent overloading yourself with carbohydrates. A diabetic diet will teach you how to balance nutrition and make good decisions.

TAKE CARE OF WHAT YOU EAT!

One of the things to do while regulating your blood sugar is to watch what you eat. The carbs and sugars in your meals have a big influence on your body, so it's critical to know what you're consuming. There are certain things to do to assist this, which I have noted below.

UNDERSTAND PORTION CONTROL.

Portion control requires selecting meals at a healthy size. To properly regulate your blood sugar, you must have control over what you consume. Portion management may assist you in losing weight, digesting meals more smoothly, staying energetic, and reducing your consumption of troublesome foods. According to the American Diabetes Association, your meals should include fewer carbohydrates, lean meats, and non-starchy veggies.

SOME FOODS AND BEVERAGES SHOULD BE AVOIDED.

To help your healthy eating journey, restrict the following foods and beverages:

- Sodium-rich foods
- Sweets (ice cream, baked goods, and candy)
- fried foods with a lot of trans fat and saturated fat
- Sugar-sweetened beverages (sodas, energy drinks, and juice)

I recommend that you consume water instead of sugary drinks. Consider using a sugar replacement in your meals as well. Tomatoes, stevia, neotame, and acesulfame potassium are examples of healthy sugar alternatives. Avoid aspartame and sucralose, which are harmful to your health.

Please abstain from alcohol if possible. However, if you must consume alcohol, do it in moderation. Men should not exceed two drinks, while women should not exceed one drink. Alcohol may cause low or high blood sugar levels; it is best avoided. Also, avoid carb-heavy beverages such as wine and beer.

BREAKFAST RECIPES

AIR FRIED EGGS

Preparation time: 15 minutes
Time to cook: 15 minutes.
4 servings
Ingredients:

- 4 eggs
- 2 cups baby spinach, washed
- 1 tablespoon olive oil (extra virgin)
- 1/2 ounces of shredded reduced-fat cheddar cheese
- Sliced bacon
- A pinch of salt
- A dash of pepper

Directions:

Preheat the air fryer to 350 degrees Fahrenheit. Warm the oil in a skillet over medium-high heat. Cook until the spinach has wilted. Remove any surplus liquid. Fill four buttered ramekins halfway with cooked spinach. Fill each ramekin with a piece of bacon, an egg, and cheese. Season with salt and pepper to taste. Place the ramekins in the Air Fryer's cooking basket. 15 minutes in the oven

Nutrition:

105.5 calories, 9.5 grammes of carbohydrates, 3 grammes of fat, 9.5 grammes of protein, and 1.2 grammes of fibre.

PANCAKES WITH CINNAMON

Preparation time: 15 minutes
Time to cook: 16 minutes.
Ingredients:

- 4 servings
- Ingredients:
- 2 eggs
- 2 cups low-fat cream cheese
- 1/2 teaspoons of cinnamon
- 1 pack of stevia

Directions:

Heat the air fryer to 330°F. In a blender, combine the cream cheese, cinnamon, eggs, and stevia. 1/4 of the mixture should be placed in the air fryer basket. Cook each side for 2 minutes. Repeat with the remainder of the mixture. Serve

Nutrition: 105.7 calories, 9.5 grammes of carbohydrates, 3.2 grammes of fat, 1.2 grammes of fiber, and 9.5 grammes of protein

SCRAMBLED EGGS

Preparation time: 5 minutes
Time to cook: 5 minutes.
2 servings
Ingredients:

- Four huge eggs
- 1/2 cup sharp shredded Cheddar
- 2 tablespoons of unsalted butter, melted

Directions:

Whisk the eggs in a 2-cup circular baking dish. Insert the dish into the air fryer basket. Set the oven temperature to 400°F and the timer for 10 minutes. After 5 minutes, whisk in the eggs, butter, and cheese. Allow it to simmer for 3 minutes before stirring again. Allow the eggs to continue cooking for another 2 minutes, or remove them when done to your preference. Fluff with a fork. Serve hot.

Nutrition: 358.3 calories, 19.8 grammes of protein, 0 grammes of fiber, 27.2 grammes of fat, and 0.9 grammes of carbohydrates

FRITTATA WITH FENNEL

Preparation time: 5 minutes
Time to cook: 15 minutes.
6 servings
Ingredients:
- 1 fennel bulb, shredded
- 6 whisked eggs
- 2 teaspoons of cilantro, chopped
- 1 teaspoon paprika dulce
- Spray cooking oil
- a dash of black pepper and salt

Directions:
In a mixing bowl, combine all of the ingredients except the cooking spray and toss thoroughly. Grease a baking pan with cooking spray, then pour in the frittata mixture and distribute it evenly. Place the pan in the air fryer and cook for 15 minutes at 370°F. Serve for breakfast on individual plates.

Nutrition:
199.2 calories, 11.4 grammes of fat, 1 grammes of fiber, 4.7 grammes of carbohydrates, and 8.4 grammes of protein

OATMEAL WITH STRAWBERRIES

Preparation time: 5 minutes
Time to cook: 15 minutes.
4 servings
Ingredients:
- 1/2 cups of shredded coconut
- 1/4 cup berries
- 2.c. coconut milk
- 1/4 teaspoons of vanilla extract
- 2 tablespoons stevia
- Spray cooking oil.

Directions:
Grease the Air Fryer's skillet with cooking spray, then add all of the ingredients and stir. Cook for 15 minutes at 365oF, then divide into bowls and serve.

Nutrition:
141.3 calories, 6.4 grammes of fat, 2 grammes of fiber, 2.8 grammes of carbohydrates, and 5.4 grammes of protein

Frittata with Mushrooms and Cheese

Time to prepare: 20 minutes.
Time to cook: 20 minutes.
4 servings
Ingredients:

- 6 eggs
- 6 cup button mushrooms, finely sliced
- 1 red onion, thinly sliced into rounds
- 6 tbsp. crumbled Feta cheese, reduced fat.
- A pinch of salt
- 2 tablespoons of olive oil.

Directions:
Heat the air fryer to 330°F. Onions and mushrooms should be sautéed. Using a paper towel, transfer it to a plate. Meanwhile, whisk the eggs in a mixing basin. Season with salt and pepper to taste. Spray a baking dish with nonstick cooking spray. Pour in the egg mixture. Mix in the mushrooms and onions. Crumbled feta cheese on top. Insert a baking dish into the air fryer basket. Cooking time is 20 minutes. Serve

Nutrition:
139.2 calories, 5.6 grammes of carbohydrates, 10.4 grammes of fat, 22.9 grammes of protein, and 1.2 grammes of fibre.

Pancakes with Cinnamon and Cheese

Time to prepare: 5-7 minutes.
Time to cook: 16 minutes.
4 servings
Ingredients:

- 2 eggs
- 2 cups low-fat cream cheese
- 1/2 teaspoons of cinnamon
- 1 pack of stevia

Directions:
Heat the air fryer to 330°F. Meanwhile, in a blender, mix the cream cheese, cinnamon, eggs, and stevia. 1/4 of the mixture should be placed in the air fryer basket. Cook each side for 2 minutes. Repeat with the remainder of the mix. Serve

Nutrition:
139.2 calories, 5.2 grammes of carbohydrates, 10.4 grammes of fat, 22.9 grammes of protein, and 1.2 grammes of fibre.

EGGS HARD-BOILED

Time to prepare: 2 minutes.
Time to cook: 15 minutes.
6 eggs per serving.
Ingredients:
- Six whole eggs

Directions:
Arrange raw eggs on the rack of your air fryer, leaving enough room for the surrounding air to circulate. In a 260°F fryer, cook the eggs for 15 minutes. Remove the boiled eggs from the fryer and place them in a basin filled with cold water for 10 minutes.

Nutrition:
3.8 g of fat, and 6.3 g of protein.

FRITTATA WITH WHITE EGGS AND SPINACH

Time to prepare: 12-15 minutes
Time to cook: 12 minutes.
4 servings
Ingredients:
- 8 beaten egg whites.
- 2 cups of spinach, fresh
- 2 tablespoons of olive oil.
- 1 green pepper, chopped
- 1 red pepper, chopped
- 1/2 cup reduced fat crumbled feta cheese
- 1/4 yellow onion, chopped
- 1 teaspoon sea salt
- 1 teaspoon black pepper

Directions:
Preheat the air fryer to 330°F. Meanwhile, fry the red, green, and yellow peppers and onions in the air fryer basket for 3 minutes. Season with salt and pepper to taste. Cook for 4 minutes after adding the egg whites. Serve with the spinach and feta cheese on top. 5 minutes in the oven Transfer to a serving platter, slice, and serve.

Nutrition:
119.5 calories, 12.4 g carbs, 4.2 g fat, 10.2 g protein, and 1.2 g fiber.

SANDWICH WITH SCALLIONS

Preparation time: 10 minutes
Time to cook: 10 minutes.
1 serving
Ingredients:
- 2 whole wheat bread slices
- 2 tablespoons of low-fat butter
- 2 scallions, finely sliced
- 1 tablespoon grated parmesan
- 3/4 cups of reduced-fat grated cheddar cheese

Directions:
Preheat the oven to 356 degrees Fahrenheit. On a piece of bread, spread butter. Place the butter side down in the frying basket. Garnish with cheese and scallions. Place the second piece of bread on top of the sandwich and top with the remaining butter and parmesan cheese. 10 minutes in the oven

Nutrition:
153.5 calories, 8.7 grammes of carbohydrates, 2.3 grammes of fat, 8.9 grammes of protein, and 2.4 grammes of fibre.

BACON IN THE AIR FRYER

Time to prepare: 2 minutes.
Time to cook: 10 minutes.
5 servings
Ingredients:
- 5 thick-cut bacon pieces.

Directions:
To cook, place the bacon pieces in the air fryer basket at least 1 inch apart. 390°F for the air fryer. Cook the bacon for 10 minutes, or until it is crispy. Before serving, drain on a kitchen napkin.

Nutrition:
102.7 calories, 2.5g fat, 0.4g carbs, 0g fibre, 0g sugar, 8.3g protein.

SANDWICHES WITH GRILLED CHEESE

Time to prepare: 2 minutes.
Time to cook: 7 minutes.
2 sandwiches per serving.
Ingredients:
- 4 slices of American cheese
- 4 sliced bread slices.
- Butter, pat

Directions:
Preheat your air fryer to 360°F. Place two slices of American cheese in the middle of two bread pieces. Spread an equal amount of butter on each side of the sandwich and place it in a single layer in the tray of your air fryer. To seal the sandwiches, place toothpicks in the corners. Cook for 4 minutes, turning once, and then cook for another 3 minutes until toasted.

Nutrition:
296.8 calories, 14.4 grammes of fat, 30.7 grammes of carbohydrates, 1 grammes of fiber, 6.8 grammes of sugar, and 12.1 grammes of protein

OMELET WITH ASPARAGUS

Preparation time: 10 minutes
Time to cook: 8 minutes.
2 servings
Ingredients:
- 3 eggs
- 5 steamed asparagus tips
- 2 tablespoons of warm milk.
- 1 tbsp. grated parmesan cheese
- Season with salt and pepper to taste.
- Cooking spray that is nonstick

Directions:
In a large mixing bowl, combine the eggs, cheese, milk, salt, and pepper. Coat a baking sheet with nonstick cooking spray. Place the pan into the baking basket after adding the asparagus mixture to the pan. For 8 minutes, preheat the air fryer to 320°F. Serve hot.

Nutrition:
230.2 calories, 9 g fat, 7.8 g carbs, and 12.4 g protein.

OMELET ORIENTAL

Preparation time: 10 minutes
Time to cook: 24 min.
1 serving
Ingredients:
- 1/2 cup fresh Shimeji mushrooms, sliced
- 2 whisked eggs.
- Season with salt and pepper to taste.
- 1 garlic clove, minced
- A handful of thinly sliced tofu
- 2 tbsp onion, coarsely chopped
- Spray cooking oil on

Directions:
Coat the baking dish with nonstick cooking spray. Mix in the onions and garlic. air fried for 4 minutes at 355°F in a preheated air fryer. Add the tofu and mushrooms to the onions and season with salt and pepper to taste. Whisk the eggs together and pour over the tofu and mushrooms. Air fried for another 20 minutes. Serve hot.

Nutrition:
209.5 calories, 10.5g fat, 8.4g carbs, and 12.9g protein.

CRISPY AVOCADO FRIES FOR BREAKFAST

Preparation time: 10 minutes
Time to cook: 6 minutes.
2 servings
Ingredients:
- Two beaten eggs
- Each cut into 8 slices
- 1/4 teaspoon black pepper
- 1/2 teaspoons of cayenne pepper
- Season with salt to taste.
- 1/2 oz. lemon juice
- 1/2 cup whole wheat flour
- 1 cup whole-wheat breadcrumbs
- Greek yoghurt to serve

Directions:
Mix in the flour, salt, pepper, and cayenne pepper. In a separate dish, combine the bread crumbs. In a third dish, whisk together the eggs. Dredge the avocado slices in the flour

mixture first. After that, dip them in the egg mixture and then in the breadcrumbs. Fill the air fryer basket halfway with avocado fries. Preheat the air fryer to 390 degrees Fahrenheit. Cook for 6 minutes using the air fryer basket in the air fryer. When the cooking time is over, place the avocado fries on a serving plate. Serve with Greek yoghurt and a drizzle of lemon juice.

Nutrition:
271.5 calories, 12.9 grammes of fat, 10.8 grammes of carbohydrates, and 15.9 grammes of protein

FRITTATA FOR BREAKFAST

Preparation time: 10 minutes
Time to cook: 10 minutes.
3 servings
Ingredients:
- 6 eggs
- Eight halved cherry tomatoes
- 2 tbsp. shredded parmesan cheese.
- 1 pound Italian sausage, chopped
- Season with salt and pepper to taste.

Directions:
Pre-heat your air fryer to 355 degrees Fahrenheit. Fill the baking dish halfway with tomatoes and meat. Cook for 5 minutes in the air fryer with the baking dish. Meanwhile, whisk together the eggs, salt, pepper, cheese, and oil in a mixing dish. Remove the baking dish from the air fryer and evenly sprinkle the egg mixture on top. Return the dish to the air fryer and bake for another 5 minutes. Remove them from the air fryer and cut them into wedges before serving.

Nutrition:
271.8 calories, 7.8 g fat, 6.7 g carbs, 13.8 g protein.

BREAKFAST MINI CHEESEBURGER SLIDERS

Preparation time: 10 minutes
Time to cook: 10 minutes.
6 servings
Ingredients:
- 1 pound beef ground
- Cheddar cheese, 6 oz.
- 6 Dinner rolls
- To taste, season with salt and black pepper.

Directions:
Pre-heat your air fryer to 390 degrees Fahrenheit. Season 6 beef patties with salt and black pepper. Cook the burger patties for 10 minutes in the frying basket. Remove the burger patties from the air fryer, cover them with cheese, and return them to the air fryer for another minute of cooking. Remove the burgers and place them on dinner rolls to serve them warm.

Nutrition:
261.7 calories, 9.2 g fat, 7.8 g carbs, and 16.8 g protein.

ROLLS WITH BACON AND CHEESE

Time to prepare: 8-10 minutes.
Time to cook: 10 minutes.
4 servings
Ingredients:
- 1 pound shredded cheddar cheese
- 1 pound rashers bacon
- 8 oz. Pillsbury Crescent Dough

Directions:
Preheat the air fryer to 330°F. Cut the bacon rashers into 1/4-inch strips and combine them with the cheddar cheese. Place aside. Cut the dough sheet into 1-inch-by-1.5-inch pieces. Place an equal quantity of the bacon and cheese mixture in the middle of each dough piece, and then squeeze the corners together to contain the filling. Place the packages in the Air Fryer basket and bake at 330°F for 7 minutes. Bake for 3 minutes more after increasing the temperature to 390°F. Serve hot.

Nutrition:
231.3 calories, 7.4 g fat, 5.5 g carbs, and 13.3 g protein.

APPETIZER AND SIDES RECIPES

CHIPS WITH GARLIC AND KALE

Preparation time: 67 minutes
Time to cook: 5 minutes.
2 servings
Ingredients:
- 1 tablespoon flakes yeast
- To taste, sea salt
- 4 cups of kale, packed
- 2 tablespoons of olive oil.
- 1 tsp. minced garlic
- 1/2 cup ranch seasoning chunks

Directions:
1. Combine the oil, greens, garlic, and ranch seasoning in a mixing dish.
2. Mix in the yeast well. Cook the coated kale in an air fryer basket for 5 minutes at 375°F.
3. After 3 minutes, shake and serve.

Nutrition:
- 50 calories
- Total fat: 1.9 g
- Carbs: 10 g
- Protein content: 46 g

BALLS OF SALMON AND GARLIC

Preparation time: 67 minutes
Time to cook: 10 minutes.
2 servings
Ingredients:
- Six ounces canned salmon
- 1 big egg
- 3 tablespoons of olive oil.
- 5 tablespoons of wheat germ.
- a half teaspoon garlic powder
- 1 tablespoon chopped fresh dill

- 4 tablespoons chopped spring onion
- 4 tbsp. diced celery.

Directions:
1. Preheat your air fryer to 370 degrees Fahrenheit. In a large mixing bowl, combine the salmon, egg, celery, onion, dill, and garlic.
2. In the wheat germ, roll the mixture into golf ball-sized balls. Warm the olive oil in a small saucepan over medium-low heat. Add the salmon balls and flatten them gradually. Place them in the air fryer and cook for 10 minutes.

Nutrition:
- 219 calories
- Total fat: 7.7 g
- Carbs: 14.8 g.
- Protein content: 23.1 g

ONIONS RINGS

Preparation time: 7 minutes
Time to cook: 10 minutes.
3 servings
Ingredients:
- 1 onion, cut into slices and then into rings.
- 1 1/2 pounds almond flour
- 3/4 cup of fried pork rinds
- 1 cup of milk
- 1 egg
- 1 tbsp. baking powder
- 1/2 teaspoon of salt.

Directions:
1. Before using your air fryer, preheat it for 10 minutes. Cut the onion into slices, then into rings. Add the flour, baking powder, and salt to a container.
2. In a mixing bowl, combine the eggs, milk, and flour. Dip the floured onion rings gently into the batter to coat.
3. Arrange the pork rinds on a platter and coat the rings with the crumbs. 4. Cook the onion rings in the air fryer for 10 minutes at 360°F.

Nutrition:
- 304 calories
- Total fat: 18g, Carbs: 31g
- 38g protein

FRIES WITH CRISPY EGGPLANT

Preparation time: 7 minutes
Time to cook: 12 minutes.
3 servings
Ingredients:
- Two eggplants
- ¼ tablespoon extra-virgin olive oil
- ¼ teaspoon almond flour
- ½ cup of water

Directions:
1. Preheat your air fryer to 390 degrees Fahrenheit. Slice the eggplant into 1/2-inch chunks. Combine the flour, olive oil, water, and eggplant in a mixing bowl.
2. Slowly coat the eggplants. Cook the eggplants in the air fryer for 12 minutes. Serve with yoghurt or tomato sauce on the side.

Nutrition:
- 103 calories
- Total fat: 7.3 g
- Carbs: 12.3 g.
- Protein: 1.9 g

BELL PEPPERS CHARRED

Preparation time: 7 minutes
Time to cook: 4 minutes.
3 servings
Ingredients:
- Twenty sliced and seeded bell peppers
- 1 tablespoon extra-virgin olive oil
- 1 teaspoon sea salt
- 1 lemon
- Pepper

Directions:
- Preheat your air fryer to 390 degrees Fahrenheit. Season the peppers with salt and oil. Cook the peppers for 4 minutes in the air fryer.
- Place the peppers in a large mixing basin and drizzle with lemon juice. Season with salt and pepper to taste.

Nutrition:
- 30 calories
- Total fat: 0.25 g
- Carbs: 6.91 g.
- Protein: 1.28 g

STEW WITH MUSHROOMS

Preparation time: 7 minutes
Cooking time is 1 hour and 22 minutes.
3 servings
Ingredients:
- 1 pound boneless, skinless chicken cubes
- 2 tbsp of canola oil
- 1 pound sliced fresh mushrooms
- 1 tablespoon thyme dried
- 1/4 cups of water
- Two tbsp tomato paste
- 4 minced garlic cloves.
- 1 cup green peppers, chopped
- 3 cups thinly sliced zucchini
- 1 large onion, sliced
- 1 teaspoon basil
- 1 tablespoon fresh marjoram
- 1 tablespoon dried oregano

Directions:

1. Cut up the chicken into cubes. Place them in the air fryer basket and drizzle with olive oil. Combine the mushrooms, zucchini, onion, and green pepper in a mixing bowl. Cook for 2 minutes before adding tomato paste, water, and spices.

2. Cook the stew for 50 minutes in the air fryer. Cook for a further 20 minutes after increasing the heat to 340oF.

3. Remove from the air fryer and transfer to a large pan. Pour in some water and cook for 10 minutes.

Nutrition:
- 53 calories
- Total fat: 3.3 g
- 4.9 g carbohydrate
- Protein: 2.3 g

CHEESE AND ONION NUGGETS

Preparation time: 7 minutes
Time to cook: 12 minutes.
4 servings
Ingredients:
- 7 oz. grated Edam cheese.
- 2 spring onions, diced
- 1 egg, beaten
- 1 teaspoon of coconut oil
- 1 tablespoon thyme dried
- Season with salt and pepper to taste.

Directions:
1. In a mixing bowl, combine the onion, cheese, coconut oil, salt, pepper, and thyme. Form eight little balls with the cheese in the middle.
2. Refrigerate for approximately an hour. Brush the beaten egg over the nuggets with a pastry brush. Cook for 12 minutes at 350oF in an air fryer.

Nutrition:
- 227 calories
- 17.3 g total fat
- Carbohydrates: 4.5 g
- Protein content: 14.2 g

NUTS WITH SPICES

Preparation time: 7 minutes
Time to cook: 25 minutes.
3 servings
Ingredients:
- One cup of almonds
- 1 cup pecan halves
- 1 cup of cashew nuts
- 1 egg white, beaten
- 1/2 teaspoon cinnamon powder
- 1 tablespoon cayenne pepper
- 1/4 tablespoon ground cloves
- A pinch of salt

Directions:
1. Combine the egg white and seasonings. your air fryer to 300 degrees Fahrenheit.

2. Combine the nuts with the spicy mixture. Cook for 25 minutes, stirring frequently throughout that time.

Nutrition:
- 88.4 calories
- Total fat: 7.6 g
- Carb 3.9 g
- Protein: 2.5 g

FRENCH FRIES MADE WITH KETONES

Time to Prepare: 7 minutes
Time to cook: 20 minutes.
4 servings
Ingredients:
- 1 large rutabaga, peeled and sliced into 14-inch spears
- Season with salt and pepper to taste.
- paprika, 1/2 teaspoon
- 2 tablespoons of coconut oil.

Directions:
1. Preheat your air fryer to 450 degrees F. Combine the oil, paprika, salt, and pepper in a mixing bowl.
2. Pour the oil mixture over the rutabaga fries, being careful to coat all of them. Cook for 20 minutes in the air fryer, or until crispy.

Nutrition:
- 113 calories
- Total fat: 7.2 g
- 12.5 g carbohydrates
- Protein: 1.9 g

GREEN GARLIC TOMATOES FRIED

Preparation time: 7 minutes
Time to cook: 12 minutes.
2 servings
Ingredients:
- Three sliced green tomatoes
- ½ cup of almond flour
- Two beaten eggs
- Season with salt and pepper to taste.

- 1 tsp. minced garlic

Directions:
1. Season the tomatoes with salt, garlic powder, and pepper to taste. 2. Pre-heat your air fryer to 400 degrees Fahrenheit. Dip the tomatoes in flour first, then in the egg mixture.
2. Brush the tomato rounds lightly with oil and place them in the air fryer basket. Cook for 8 minutes, then turn over and cook for 4 minutes more. With keto mayonnaise, serve.

Nutrition:
- 123 calories
- Total fat: 3.9 g
- Carbohydrates: 16 g.
- Protein content: 8.4 g

TOTS WITH GARLIC AND CAULIFLOWER

Preparation time: 7 minutes
Time to cook: 20 minutes.
4 servings
Ingredients:
- 1 cauliflower crown, finely chopped
- 1/2 cup parmesan cheese, grated
- Season with salt and pepper to taste.
- 1/4 cup of almond flour
- 2 eggs
- 1 tsp. minced garlic

Directions:
1. Combine all of the ingredients and shape them. Into tots and coat with olive oil. Pre-heat your air fryer to 400 degrees Fahrenheit.
2. Cook each side for 10 minutes.

Nutrition:
- 18 calories
- Total fat: 0.6 g
- 1.3 g carbohydrate
- Protein content: 1.8 g

POULTRY RECIPES

SALAD WITH WARM CHICKEN AND SPINACH

Preparation time: 10 minutes
Time to cook: 16-20 minutes.
4 servings
Ingredients:
- 3 low-sodium boneless, skinless chicken breasts (5 oz.)
- Cubes of 1 inch.
- 5 tablespoons of olive oil
- a half teaspoon dried thyme
- 1 medium red onion, chopped
- 1 red bell pepper, sliced
- 1 thinly sliced small zucchini
- 3 tbsp freshly squeezed lemon juice
- 6 cups of baby spinach, fresh

Directions:
1. In a large mixing bowl, combine the chicken, olive oil, and thyme. To coat, toss everything together. Transfer to a medium metal bowl and cook in the air fryer for 8 minutes.
2. Combine the red onion, bell pepper, and zucchini in a mixing bowl. Roast for 8 to 12 minutes longer, tossing once, or until the chicken reaches an internal temperature of 165°F on a meat thermometer.
   Remove the air fryer dish from the oven and whisk in the lemon juice.
3. Toss the spinach with the chicken mixture in a serving dish. Toss everything together and serve right away.

Nutrition:
- 214 calories
- Fat: 7 g (29% of calories from fat) (29% of calories from fat)
- Saturated fat: 1 g
- Protein content: 28 g
- 7 g carbohydrate
- 116 milligrams of sodium
- 2 g dietary fibre

CRISPY CHICKEN WINGS IN A PAIR

Preparation time: 10 minutes
Time to cook: 18 minutes.
4 servings
Ingredients:
- 12 different chicken scenes
- 1/2 cup of chicken broth.
- Season with salt and black pepper to taste.

1 tbsp. melted butter

Directions:
1. Place a metal rack in the air fryer oven and pour in the broth.
2. Arrange the pieces on the metal rack, and then close the pressure cooker lid. 3.
3. Press the "Pressure Button," choose 8 minutes of cooking time, and then press "Start."
4. When the air fryer oven beeps, perform a quick release and remove the cover.
5. Arrange the cooked vignettes in a dish.
6. Remove the saucepan from the oven and place an air fryer basket inside.
7. Toss the vignettes in a bowl with the butter and spices.
8. 8. Arrange the prepared pieces in the air-fryer basket.
9. 9. Place the cover on the pan and press the "Air Fryer Button," then set the timer for 10 minutes.
10. 10. Remove the cover with care and serve.

11. Enjoy!

Nutrition:
- 246 calories
- Total fat: 18.9 g
- Saturated Fat: 7g
- 115mg of cholesterol
- 149mg sodium
- 0 g of Total Carbohydrates
- 0 g of dietary fibre
- Total sugars: 0 g
- Protein content: 20.2 g

THE WHOLE ITALIAN CHICKEN

Preparation time: 10 minutes
Time to cook: 35 minutes.
4 servings
Ingredients:
- 1 whole chicken
- 2 tbsp. of your preferred oil spray.
- 1 tablespoon garlic powder
- 1 tsp. onion powder
- 1 paprika teaspoon
- 1 teaspoon of Italian seasoning
- 2 tablespoons of Montreal steak seasoning.
- 1 1/2 cups of chicken broth

Directions:
1. In a dish, combine all of the ingredients and rub over the chicken.
2. Place a metal rack in the air fryer oven and pour in the broth.
3. Place the chicken on the metal rack in the pressure cooker and cover with the lid.
4. Press the "Pressure Button" and set the timer for 25 minutes, then press "Start."
5. When the air fryer oven sounds, make a natural release and take the top off.
6. Place the pressure-cooked chicken on a platter.
7. 7. Remove the saucepan from the oven and insert the air fryer basket.
8. 8. Toss the chicken pieces in the oil to thoroughly coat.
9. 9. Arrange the seasoned chicken in the air fryer basket.
10. Place the cover on the pan and press the "Air Fryer Button," then set the timer for 10 minutes.
11. Remove the cover with care and serve.
12. Enjoy!

Nutrition:
- 163 calories
- Total fat: 10.7 g
- Saturated fat: 2 g
- 33 milligrams of cholesterol
- 1439 milligrams sodium
- 1.8 g carbohydrate
- 0.3 g of dietary fibre
- Total sugars: 0.8 g
- Protein: 12.6 g

POT PIE WITH CHICKEN

Preparation time: 10 minutes
Time to cook: 17 minutes.
3 servings
Ingredients:
- 2 tablespoons of olive oil.
- 1 pound chicken breast, diced
- 1 teaspoon garlic powder
- 1 teaspoon thyme
- 1 teaspoon black pepper
- 1 cup chicken broth
- 12 oz. frozen mixed vegetables
- Four large diced potatoes
- 10 oz. can of creamed chicken soup.
- 1 cup of heavy cream

Directions:
1. Preheat the air fryer oven to "Sauté" and add the chicken and olive oil.
2. Cook for 5 minutes before adding the seasonings to the chicken.
3. Combine the broth, vegetables, and cream of chicken soup in a mixing bowl.
4. Place the pressure-cooking cover on top and seal it.
5. Press the "Pressure Button," then pick 10 minutes of cooking time before pressing "Start."
6. When the air fryer oven sounds, make a rapid release and take the top off.
7. Take off the cover and mix in the cream.
8. Press the "Sauté" button for 2 minutes.
9. Enjoy!

Nutrition:
- 568 calories
- Total fat: 31.1 g
- Saturated fat: 9.1 g
- 95 milligrams of cholesterol
- 1111 milligrams of sodium
- 50.8 g total carbohydrates
- g of dietary fibre
- Total sugars: 18.8 g
- Protein content: 23.4 g

Chicken Casserole

Preparation time: 10 minutes
Time to cook: 9 minutes.
4 servings
Ingredients:
- 12 oz. bag egg noodles
- 1/2 large onion
- 1/2 cup chopped carrots
- One-quarter cup frozen peas
- 1/4 cup frozen chopped broccoli
- 2 celery stalks, chopped
- 5 cup chicken broth
- 1 tablespoon garlic powder
- Season with salt and pepper to taste.
- 1 cup cheddar cheese, shredded
- 1 pound sliced French onions
- 1/4 gallon soured cream
- 1 cans mushroom-chicken cream soup

Directions:
1. In the air fryer oven, combine the chicken broth, black pepper, salt, garlic powder, veggies, and egg noodles.
2. Please close and seal the pressure-cooking cover.
3. Press the "Pressure Button," choose 4 minutes of cooking time, and then press "Start."
4. When the air fryer oven beeps, perform a quick release and remove the cover.
5. Stir in the cheese, a third of the French onions, a can of soup, and the sour cream.
6. Gently fold in the remaining onion and serve.
7. Close and seal the air fryer's cover.
8. Click the "Air Fryer Button" and set the timer for 5 minutes, then press "Start."
9. When the Air Fryer oven beeps, remove the cover.
10. Serve

Nutrition:
- 494 calories
- Total fat: 19.1 g
- Saturated fat: 9.6 g
- 142 mg of cholesterol
- 1233 milligrams sodium
- 29 g total carbohydrates
- g of dietary fibre

- Total sugar: 3.7 g
- Protein, 48.9 g.

MACARONI AND CHEESE WITH CHICKEN

Preparation time: 10 minutes
Time to cook: 9 minutes.
4 servings
Ingredients:
- 2 ½ cup of macaroni
- 2 cup chicken stock
- 1 cup cooked shredded chicken
- 1 quart heavy cream
- 8 tablespoons of butter
- 1 bag Ritz crackers

Directions:
1. In the air fryer oven Duo, combine the chicken stock, heavy cream, chicken, 4 tablespoons of butter, and macaroni.
2. Place the pressure-cooking cover on top and seal it.
3. Press the "Pressure Button," choose 4 minutes of cooking time, and then press "Start."
4. Crush the crackers and thoroughly combine them with 4 tablespoons of melted butter.
5. When the air fryer oven sounds, execute a rapid release and take the top off.
6. Replace and seal the cover.
7. Press the "Air Fryer Button" and choose 5 minutes of cooking time before pressing "Start."
8. When the air fryer oven beeps, remove the cover.
9. Serve

Nutrition:
- 611 calories
- Total fat: 43.6 g
- 26.8 g of saturated fat.
- 147 milligrams of cholesterol
- 739 milligrams sodium
- 29.5 g total carbohydrates
- 1.2 g of dietary fibre
- Total sugar: 1.7 g
- Protein content: 25.4 g

CASSEROLE WITH BROCCOLI AND CHICKEN

Preparation time: 10 minutes
Time to cook: 22 min.
4 servings
Ingredients:
- 1 ½ cup of chicken cubes
- 2 tsp. minced garlic.
- 2 tablespoons of butter.
- 1 1/2-cup chicken stock
- 1 ½ cup long-grain rice
- 1 (10.75 oz.) can of creamed chicken soup.
- 2 cups broccoli florets
- 1 cup crushed Ritz crackers
- 2 tbsp. softened butter
- 2 cups shredded cheddar cheese
- 1 cup of water

Directions:
1. Place a basket inside the air fryer oven Duo and fill it with 1 cup of water.
2. Distribute the broccoli equally in the basket.
1. Place the pressure-cooking cover on top and seal it.
3. Press the "Pressure Button," choose 1 minute of cooking time, and then press "Start."
4. When the air fryer oven sounds, execute a rapid release and take the top off.
5. Remove the broccoli from the Duo air fryer oven.
6. Press the "Sauté" button and add 2 tablespoons of butter.
7. Add the chicken and cook for 5 minutes, then add the garlic and cook for 30 seconds more.
8. In a mixing bowl, combine rice, chicken broth, and cream of chicken soup.
9. Place the pressure-cooking cover on top and seal it.
10. Press the "Pressure Button," then pick 12 minutes of cooking time before pressing "Start."
2. When the air fryer oven sounds, do a rapid release and remove the cover.
13. Gently fold in the cheese and broccoli.
14. Combine the crackers and 2 tablespoons of butter in a dish and distribute them over the chicken in the saucepan.
15. Replacing the cover and sealing it
16. Click the "Air Fryer Button" and set the timer for 4 minutes, then press "Start."
17. Remove the cover of the air fryer oven when it beeps.
18. Serve

Nutrition:
- 609 calories
- Total fat: 24.4 g
- Saturated fat 12.6 g
- 142 mg of cholesterol
- 924mg sodium
- 45.5 g total carbohydrates
- 1.4 g of dietary fibre
- Total sugar: 1.6 g
- Protein content: 49.2 g

TIKKA CHICKEN KEBABS

Preparation time: 10 minutes
Time to cook: 17 minutes.
4 servings
Ingredients:
- 1 pound cubed boneless skinless chicken thighs
- 1 teaspoon oil
- 1/2 cup red onion, diced
- 1/2 cup green bell pepper, diced
- 1/2 cup red bell pepper, diced
- Toppings: lime wedges and onion rounds

For the marinade:
- 1/2 yoghurt cup Greek
- 3/4 tablespoon grated ginger
- ¾ garlic clove, minced
- 1 lime juice tablespoon
- 2 teaspoons mild red chilli powder
- 1/2 tablespoon turmeric powder
- 1 tsp. garam masala
- 1 tbsp. coriander powder
- 1/2 tablespoon fenugreek leaves, dried
- 1 teaspoon sea salt

Directions:
1. Make the marinade by combining all of the ingredients in a basin.
2. Fold in the chicken and mix well to coat before placing in the refrigerator for 8 hours.
3. To the marinade, add the bell pepper, onions, and oil.
4. Thread the skewers with the chicken, peppers, and onions.

5. Place the air fryer basket in the Duo oven.
6. Replace and seal the cover.
7. Press the "Air Fryer Button," then pick 10 minutes of cooking time before pressing "Start."
8. When the air fryer oven beeps, remove the cover.
9. Flip the skewers over and cook for another 7 minutes in the air fryer.
10. Serve

Nutrition:
- 241 calories
- Total fat: 14.2 g
- Saturated fat: 3.8 g
- 92 mg of cholesterol
- 695 milligrams sodium
- 8.5 g total carbohydrates
- 1.6 g of dietary fibre
- Total sugar: 3.9 g
- Protein content: 21.8 g

CHICKEN AND BACON WRAPPED

Preparation time: 10 minutes
Time to cook: 24 min.
4 servings
Ingredients:
- 1/4 cup of maple syrup
- 1 teaspoon ground black pepper
- 1 tsp. Dijon mustard
- 1/4 teaspoons of garlic powder
- kosher salt, 1/8 teaspoon
- 4 skinless, boneless chicken breasts (6 oz.)
- 8 slices bacon

Directions:
1. In a small bowl, combine maple syrup, salt, garlic powder, mustard, and black pepper.
2. Season the chicken breasts with salt and black pepper, and then wrap each in two pieces of bacon.
3. Place the covered chicken in the baking pan of the air fryer oven.
4. Drizzle the maple syrup mixture over the covered chicken.
5. Replace and seal the cover.

6. Press the "Bake Button" and choose 20 cooking times before pressing "Start."
7. When the function is finished, turn to "Broil" mode and cook for 4 minutes.

8. Serve

Nutrition:
- 441 calories
- Total fat: 18.3 g
- Saturated fat: 5.2 g
- 141 milligrams of cholesterol
- 1081 milligrams of sodium
- 14 g total carbohydrates
- g of dietary fibre
- Total sugars: 11.8 g
- Protein content: 53.6 g

THIGHS OF CREAMY CHICKEN

Preparation time: 10 minutes
Time to cook: 30 minutes.
2 servings
Ingredients:
- 1 tablespoon extra-virgin olive oil
- 6 bone-in, skin-on chicken thighs
- Salt
- Black pepper, freshly ground.
- 3/4 cup chicken broth (low sodium).
- ½ heavy cream
- 1/2 cup sun-dried tomatoes, chopped
- 1/4 cup grated Parmesan cheese
- To serve, use freshly torn basil.

Directions:
1. In the air fryer oven, heat the oil by pressing the "Sauté Button."
2. Add the chicken, salt, and black pepper, and sear for 5 minutes on each side.
3. Combine the broth, cream, parmesan, and tomatoes in a mixing bowl.
4. Close the cover of the air fryer.
5. Select "Bake" and 20 minutes of cooking time, then hit "Start."
6. When the Air Fryer oven beeps, remove the cover.
7. Before serving, garnish with basil.

Nutrition:
- 454 calories
- Total fat: 37.8 g
- Saturated fat: 14.4g
- 169mg of cholesterol
- 181 milligrams sodium 2.8 g
- 0.7 g of dietary fibre
- Total sugars: 0.7 g
- Protein: 26.9 g

TERIYAKI HEN DRUMSTICKS IN THE AIR FRYER

Preparation time: 30 minutes
Time to cook: 20 minutes.
4 servings
Ingredients:
- Six chicken drumsticks
- 1 tbsp. teriyaki sauce.

Directions:
1. In a zip-lock bag, combine the drumsticks and teriyaki sauce. Allow the sauce to sit for 30 minutes.
2. Preheat your air fryer to 360 degrees F.
3. Place the drumsticks in the air fryer basket in a single layer and cook for 20 minutes. Shake the basket twice during meal preparation.
4. Serve with sesame seeds and sliced onions as garnish.

Nutrition:
- 163 calories
- 7 g carbohydrate
- Protein (16 g)
- Fat: 7 g

BEEF RECIPES

WRAPS FILLED WITH MEATLOAF

Preparation time: 15 minutes
Time to cook: 10 minutes.
2 servings
Ingredients:
- 1 pound ground grass-fed beef
- ½ cup of almond flour
- ¼ cup of coconut flour
- ½ tablespoon minced garlic
- 1/4 cup white onion, finely sliced
- 1 teaspoon of Italian seasoning
- ½ teaspoon of sea salt
- ½ teaspoon tarragon dried
- ½ teaspoon black pepper, ground
- 1 tablespoon of Worcestershire sauce.
- Ketchup, 1/4 cup
- 2 pastured eggs, beaten
- 1 head lettuce

Directions:
1. Toss all of the ingredients together in a mixing bowl, then shape into 2-inch diameter and 1-inch thick patties and chill for 10 minutes.
2. In the meantime, turn on the air fryer, insert the frying basket, coat it with olive oil, close the cover, and warm it for 10 minutes at 360 o F.
3. Preheat the fryer, place the patties in a single layer, shut the lid, and cook for 10 minutes, or until pleasantly browned and done, turning halfway through the cooking.
4. When the air fryer sounds, remove the patties and place them on a platter.
5. Wrap each patty in lettuce and serve.

Nutrition:
- 228 calories
- 6 g carbohydrate
- Fat: 16 g
- 13 grammes of protein

- 2 g dietary fibre

A BURGER WITH TWO CHEESES

Preparation time: 5 minutes
Time to cook: 18 minutes.
1 serving
Ingredients:
- Two pastured beef patties.
- 1/8 tablespoon onion powder
- 2 low-fat mozzarella cheese slices
- 1/8 teaspoon ground black pepper
- a quarter teaspoon of salt
- 2 tablespoons of olive oil.

Directions:
1. Preheat the air fryer to 370oF for 5 minutes, insert the basket, coat with olive oil, and close the cover.
2. In the meantime, season the patties well with onion powder, black pepper, and salt.
3. Preheat the fryer, add the beef patties, close the lid, and cook for 12 minutes, or until the patties are pleasantly browned and done, rotating halfway through.
4. Top each patty with a cheese slice and heat for 1 minute, or until the cheese melts.
5. Serve right away.

Nutrition:
- 670 calories
- 0 g carbohydrates
- Fat: 50 g
- 39 grammes of protein
- 0 g fibre

SCHNITZEL (BEEF)

Preparation time: 10 minutes
Time to cook: 15 minutes.
1 serving
Ingredients:
- 1 lean meat schnitzel
- 2 tablespoons of olive oil.
- ¼ cup of bread crumbs
- 1 egg
- To serve, 1 lemon and salad greens.

Directions:
1. Preheat the air fryer to 180 degrees Celsius.
2. In a large mixing bowl, combine breadcrumbs and oil and stir thoroughly until a crumbly mixture forms.
3. After dipping the beef steak in the whisked egg, coat it in the breadcrumb mixture.
4. Cook the breaded beef in the air fryer for 15 minutes or longer, or until thoroughly cooked through.
5. Remove from the air fryer and serve immediately with salad leaves and lemon wedges on the side.

Nutrition:
- 340 calories
- Protein (20 g)
- 14 g carbohydrates
- Fat: 10 g
- 7 grammes of fibre

BUNDLES OF STEAK WITH ASPARAGUS

Time to prepare: 20 minutes.
Time to cook: 30 minutes.
2 servings
Ingredients:
- Spray with olive oil.
- 6, 2 pound flank steak slices
- Black pepper with kosher salt.
- 2 minced garlic cloves.
- Four cups of asparagus
- Tamari sauce, 1/2 teaspoon
- 3 finely sliced bell peppers.
- 1/3 cup beef broth
- 1 tbsp. unsalted butter
- ¼ cup of balsamic vinegar

Directions:
1. Season and massage the meat with salt and pepper.
2. In a Ziploc bag, combine the garlic and Tamari sauce, then add the steak, stir well, and seal the bag.
3. Marinate it for 1 hour or overnight.
4. Distribute the bell peppers and asparagus evenly over the middle of the steak.
5. Tightly wrap the steak around the vegetables and secure with toothpicks.

6. Preheat the air fryer to high.
7. Spray the steak with olive oil. Place the steaks in the air fryer.
8. Cook for 15 minutes at 400 degrees Fahrenheit, or until the steaks are done.
9. Remove the steak from the air fryer and set it aside to rest for 5 minutes.
10. Remove the steak bundles and set them aside for 5 minutes before serving and slicing.
11. Meanwhile, heat the butter, balsamic vinegar, and broth over medium heat. Cut in half after thoroughly mixing. Season with salt and pepper to taste.
12. Drizzle over steaks just before serving.

Nutrition:
- 471 calories
- Protein content: 29 g
- 20 g carbohydrates
- Fat: 15 g

HAMBURGERS

Preparation time: 5 minutes
Time to cook: 6 minutes.
4 servings
Ingredients:
- 4 buns
- 4 cups lean ground beef chuck
- Season with salt to taste.
- 4 slivers of any cheese.
- Black pepper to taste
- 2 cut tomatoes
- 1 head lettuce
- Using ketchup as a dressing

Directions:
1. Preheat the air fryer to 350 degrees Fahrenheit.
2. In a mixing bowl, combine lean ground beef, pepper, and salt. Form patties from the mixture.
3. Cook for 6 minutes, flipping halfway through, in a single layer in the air fryer. For 1 minute before removing the patties, sprinkle with cheese.
4. Remove the cheese from the air fryer after it has melted.
5. Spread ketchup or other dressing on your buns; top with tomatoes, lettuce, and patties.
6. Serve right away.

Nutrition:
- 520 calories
- Carbohydrates: 22 g.
- Protein: 31 g
- Fat, 34 g

KABOBS OF BEEF STEAK WITH VEGETABLES

Preparation time: 30 minutes
Time to cook: 10 minutes.
4 servings
Ingredients:
- 2 tbsp soy sauce (light)
- 4 cups lean beef chuck ribs, cut up
- 1/3 cup low-fat sour cream
- 1/2 onion
- 8 skewers, 6 in.
- 1 small red bell pepper
- Pepper, black
- Dupable yoghurt

Directions:
1. Combine soy sauce and sour cream in a mixing basin. Add the lean beef pieces, coat thoroughly, and marinate for 30 minutes or longer.
2. Cube the onion and bell pepper. Soak skewers in water for 10 minutes.
3. Skewer the onions, bell peppers, and meat; season with black pepper if desired.
4. Cook for 10 minutes in a preheated air fryer at 400 o F, flipping halfway through.
5. Serve with the yoghurt dipping sauce.

Nutrition:
- 268 calories
- Protein (20 g)
- 15 g carbohydrate
- Fat: 10 g

STEAK RIB-EYE

Preparation time: 5 minutes
Time to cook: 14 minutes.
2 servings
Ingredients:
- 2 medium-sized lean ribeye steaks.
- To -taste, season with salt and freshly ground black pepper.
- Salad with micro greens to serve

Directions:
1. Preheat the air fryer to 400 degrees Fahrenheit. Using paper towels, pat dry the steaks.
2. Season steaks with any spice mixture or simply salt and pepper.
3. Apply it liberally to both sides of the meat.
4. Place steaks in the air fryer basket. Cook to the desired level of rareness. Alternatively, cook for 14 minutes and flip after half.
5. Remove from the air fryer and place on a cooling rack for 5 minutes.
6. Serve with a micro green salad.

Nutrition:
- 470 calories
- 45 grammes of protein
- Fat: 31 g
- 23 g carbohydrate

SLOPPY JOES WITHOUT MEAT

Preparation time: 15 minutes
Time to cook: 40 minutes.
2 servings
Ingredients:
- 6 large sweet potatoes
- 1 pound (454 g) lean ground beef
- 1 onion, finely chopped
- 1 carrot, finely sliced
- 1/4 cup finely chopped mushrooms
- 1/4 cup finely chopped red bell pepper
- 3 garlic cloves, minced
- 2 tbsp. Worcestershire sauce
- 1 tablespoon of white wine vinegar.
- 1 low-sodium tomato sauce cans (15 oz/425 g)
- Two tbsp tomato paste

Directions:
1. Preheat the air fryer oven to 400 degrees Fahrenheit (205 degrees Celsius).
2. Arrange the sweet potatoes in a single layer in a baking dish. Bake for 25–40 minutes (depending on size), or until tender and cooked through.
3. While the sweet potatoes are roasting, brown the meat in a large pan over medium heat, breaking it up into tiny pieces as you stir.
4. Sauté the onion, carrot, mushrooms, bell pepper, and garlic for 1 minute.
5. Combine the Worcestershire sauce, vinegar, tomato sauce, and tomato paste in a mixing bowl. Bring to a simmer, and then lower to a low heat for 5 minutes to let the flavours mingle.
6. To serve, spoon 1/2 cups of the beef mixture on top of each cooked potato.

Nutrition:
- 372 calories
- Fat: 19 g
- Protein (16 g)
- Carbohydrates: 34 g
- 13 grammes of sugar
- 6 g fibre
- 161 milligrams of sodium

"CURRY WITH BEEF"

Preparation time: 15 minutes
Time to cook: 10 minutes.
2 servings
Ingredients:
- 1 tablespoon olive oil (extra virgin)
- 1 tiny onion, finely sliced
- 2 tsp of fresh ginger, minced
- 3 garlic cloves, minced
- 2 teaspoons of ground coriander.
- 1 tsp. cumin powder
- 1 Serrano or jalapeo pepper, cut lengthwise but not through
- All the way through
- A quarter teaspoon turmeric powder
- A quarter teaspoon of salt
- Grass-fed sirloin tip steak, top round steak, or top round steak 1 pound (454 g)
- Cut sirloin steak into bite-size chunks.
- 2 tbsp. fresh cilantro, chopped

- 1/4 cups of water

Directions:
1. In an air fryer oven, heat the oil to medium-high.
2. Cook for 3 to 5 minutes, or until the onion is softened and caramelized. Stir in the ginger and garlic for approximately 30 seconds, or until fragrant.
3. Combine the coriander, cumin, jalapeo, turmeric, and salt in a small bowl.
4. Stir continually for 1 minute after adding the spice combination to the skillet. 1/4 cups of water should be used to deglaze the skillet.
5. Cook for about 5 minutes, stirring constantly, until the beef is well-browned but still medium-rare. Take out the jalapeo. Garnish with cilantro and serve.

Nutrition:
- 140 calories
- Fat: 7 g
- Protein content: 18 g
- 3 g carbohydrate
- 1 grammes sugar
- 1 grammes of fibre
- 141 milligrams of sodium

SALAD WITH ASIAN GRILLED BEEF

Preparation time: 15 minutes
Time to cook: 15 minutes.
4 servings
Ingredients:
Dressing:
- 1/4 cup freshly squeezed lime juice
- 1 tbsp gluten-free soy sauce or tamari with low sodium
- 1 tablespoon olive oil (extra virgin)
- 1 garlic clove, minced
- 1 tablespoon honey
- 1/4 teaspoons of red pepper flakes

Salad:
- 1 pound grass-fed flank steak (454 g)
- a quarter teaspoon of salt
- 1 teaspoon black pepper, freshly ground
- 6 cups of leaf lettuce, chopped
- Sliced into half-moons after being halved lengthwise

- 1 small chopped red onion
- 1 carrot, snipped into ribbons
- 1/4 cup fresh cilantro, chopped

Directions:
Prepare the salad:
- Whisk together the lime juice, tamari, olive oil, garlic, honey, and red pepper flakes in a small bowl. Place aside.

Prepare the Salad:
1. Season both sides of the meat with salt and pepper.
2. Preheat the air fryer to 400 degrees Fahrenheit (205 degrees Celsius).
3. Cook the beef for 3 to 6 minutes on each side, depending on how well done you want it. Set aside for 10 minutes, tented with aluminium foil.
4. Toss the lettuce, cucumber, onion, carrot, and cilantro in a large mixing dish.
5. Thinly slice the meat against the grain and place it in the salad dish.
6. Drizzle with the dressing and mix well. Serve

Nutrition:
- 231 calories
- Fat: 10 g
- Protein content: 26 g
- 10 g carbohydrate
- 4 g of sugar
- 2 g dietary fibre
- 349 milligrams sodium

POT ROAST ON SUNDAY

Preparation time: 10 minutes
Cooking time is 1 hour 45 minutes.
4 servings
Ingredients:
- 1 beef rump roast (3-4 pounds/1.4-1.8 kilograms)
- 2 tbsp. kosher salt, divided
- 2 tablespoons of avocado oil.
- 1 big onion, finely chopped (about 112 cups).
- 4 big carrots, chopped into 4 pieces each.
- 1 tbsp. minced garlic
- 3 cups of beef broth (low sodium)
- 1 teaspoon freshly ground black pepper

- 1 tbsp. dried parsley
- 2 tablespoons of all-purpose flour

Directions:
1. Sprinkle 1 teaspoon salt over the roast.
2. Preheat the air fryer to 400 degrees Fahrenheit (205 degrees Celsius).
3. Add the avocado oil. Place the roast in the saucepan with care and sear it for 6 to 9 minutes on each side. (A dark caramelised crust is desired.) Click "Cancel."
4. Remove the roast from the cooker and place it on a dish.
5. Add the onion, carrots, and garlic to the saucepan in that order.
6. Place the roast on top of the veggies, along with any liquid that has gathered.
7. Combine the broth, remaining 1 teaspoon salt, pepper, and parsley in a medium mixing bowl. Over the roast, pour the broth mixture.
8. Close and lock the air fryer's cover. Set the valve to the sealing position.
9. Cook on high pressure for 1 hour and 30 minutes.
10. When the cooking is finished, press "Cancel" and let the pressure drop normally.
11. When the pin falls, release and remove the lid.
12. Transfer the roast and vegetables to a serving plate using big slotted spoons while you create the gravy.
13. Remove the fat from the liquids in the saucepan using a big spoon or a fat separator. Bring the liquid to a boil in the electric pressure cooker on the "Sauté" setting.
14. To form slurry, mix together the flour and 4 tablespoons of water in a small bowl. Pour the slurry into the saucepan and whisk periodically until the gravy reaches the desired thickness. Season with salt and pepper to taste.
15. Toss the meat and carrots with the gravy and serve.

Nutrition:
- 245 calories
- Fat: 10 g
- Protein content: 33 g
- 6 g carbohydrate
- 2 g of sugar
- 1 grammes of fibre
- 397 mg/s...
-

FAJITA BOWLS WITH BEEF AND PEPPERS

Preparation time: 10 minutes
Time to cook: 15 minutes.
4 servings

Ingredients:
- 4 tbsp extra virgin olive oil
- 1 riced cauliflower head
- 1 pound (454 g) cut into 14-inch strips sirloin steak
- 1 red bell pepper, seeded and sliced
- 1 onion, finely sliced
- 2 minced garlic cloves.
- 2 squeezed limes
- 1 tsp. chilli powder

Directions:
1. Preheat the air fryer oven to 400 degrees Fahrenheit (205 degrees Celsius).
2. Heat 2 tablespoons olive oil in a small saucepan over medium heat until it shimmers.
3. Stir in the cauliflower." Cook, stirring periodically, for 3 minutes, or until it softens. Place aside.
4. Heat the remaining 2 tablespoons of oil in the air fryer on medium-high until it shimmers.
5. Cook, tossing periodically, until the meat is browned, approximately 3 minutes. Remove the steak from the skillet using a slotted spoon and set it aside.
6. Add the bell pepper and onion and mix well. Cook, stirring periodically, for approximately 5 minutes, or until they begin to brown.
7. Cook, stirring regularly, for 30 seconds after adding the garlic.
8. Return the meat to the pan, along with any liquids that have gathered, and the cauliflower. Combine the lime juice and chilli powder in a mixing bowl. Cook, stirring constantly, for 2 to 3 minutes, or until everything is well warmed.

Nutrition:
- 310 calories
- Fat: 18 g
- Protein content: 27 g
- 13 g carbohydrate
- 2 g of sugar
- 3 g dietary fibre
- The sodium content is 93 mg.

PORK RECIPES

PORK RIBS IN COUNTRY STYLE

Preparation time: 5 minutes
Cooking time: 2025 minutes
4 servings
Ingredients:
- 12 country-style pork ribs, with superfluous fat removed.
- 2 teaspoons cornstarch
- 2 tablespoons of olive oil.
- 1 tsp. dried mustard
- 1/2 teaspoon fresh thyme
- 1/2 teaspoon garlic powder
- 1 tbsp. dried marjoram
- A pinch of salt
- To taste, freshly ground black pepper.

Directions:
1. Spread the ribs out on a clean surface.
2. Combine the cornstarch, olive oil, mustard, thyme, garlic powder, marjoram, salt, and pepper in a small dish and massage into the ribs. 3.
3. Place the ribs in the air fryer basket and cook for 10 minutes at 400 degrees Fahrenheit (204 degrees Celsius).
4. Using tongs carefully flip the ribs and roast for 10 to 15 minutes, or until crisp and an internal temperature of at least 150 oF (66 oC) is registered.

Nutrition:
- 579 calories
- Fat: 44 g
- Protein content: 40 g
- 4 g carbohydrate
- 0 g fibre
- 0 g of sugar
- The sodium content is 155 mg.

Dijon Tenderloin de Pork

Preparation time: 10 minutes
Time to cook: 1214 minutes.
4 servings
Ingredients:
- 1 pound (454 g) thinly sliced pork tenderloin
- A pinch of salt
- To taste, freshly ground black pepper.
- 2 tablespoons Dijon mustard
- 1 garlic clove, minced
- a half teaspoon dried basil
- 1 cup freshly made bread crumbs
- 2 tablespoons of olive oil.

Directions:
1. Pinch the pork pieces until they are about 3/4 inches thick. Season with salt and pepper. Both sides with salt and pepper.
2. Season the pork with garlic and basil after brushing it with Dijon mustard.
3. In a mixing bowl, combine the bread crumbs and olive oil. Pat the pork pieces dry after coating them with the bread crumb mixture.
4. Arrange the pork in the air fryer basket, allowing room between each piece. Air fried for 12 to 14 minutes at 390oF (199oC), or until the pork registers 145oF (63oC) on a meat thermometer and the coating is crisp and golden. Serve immediately.

Nutrition:
- 336 calories
- Fat: 13 g
- Protein content: 34 g
- 20 g carbohydrates
- 2 g dietary fibre
- 2 g of sugar
- 390 milligrams sodium

Satay Pork

Preparation time: 15 minutes
Time to cook: 914 minutes
4 servings
Ingredients:
- 1 pound (454 g) of pork tenderloin, diced into 1 1/2-inch cubes.
- 1/4 cup of onion, minced
- 2 minced garlic cloves.
- 1 jalapeo pepper, minced
- 2 tbsp freshly squeezed lime juice
- 2 tablespoons of coconut milk.
- 2 tablespoons of unsweetened peanut butter.
- 2 tablespoons curry powder

Directions:
1. In a medium mixing bowl, combine the pork, onion, garlic, jalapeo, lime juice, coconut milk, peanut butter, and curry powder. Allow it to stand at room temperature for 10 minutes.
2. Remove the pork from the marinade using a slotted spoon.
3. Keep the marinade aside.
4. Skewer the meat on 8 bamboo or metal skewers. Air fry the pork at 380oF (193oC) for 9 to 14 minutes, brushing once with the remaining marinade, until it registers 145oF (63oC) on a meat thermometer. Remove any leftover marinade. Serve immediately.

Nutrition:
- 195 calories
- Fat: 7 g
- Protein content: 25 g
- 7 g carbohydrate
- 1 grammes of fibre
- 3 g of sugar
- 65 milligrams of sodium

AIR FRYER PORK TAQUITOS

Preparation time: 10 minutes
Time to cook: 7-10 minutes.
2 servings
Ingredients:
- 3 cups shredded cooked pork tenderloin
- Spray cooking oil on
- 2 ½ fat-free shredded mozzarella
- 10 mini tortillas.
- 1 tsp lime juice

Directions:
1. Preheat the air fryer to 380 degrees Fahrenheit.
2. Combine the lime juice and the meat.
3. To soften the tortilla, microwave it for 10 seconds with a moist cloth over it.
4. Place the pork filling and cheese on top of a tortilla and wrap it up firmly.
5. Arrange tortillas on a foil-lined baking sheet.
6. Spray the tortillas with oil. Cook for 7 to 10 minutes, or until golden brown, flipping halfway through.
7. Serve with a fresh salad on the side.

Nutrition:
- 253 calories
- Fat: 18 g
- 10 g carbohydrate
- Protein (20 g)

DELECTABLE EGG ROLLS

Preparation time: 10 minutes
Time to cook: 20 minutes.
3 servings
Ingredients:
- 1/2 coleslaw mix bag
- 1/2 onion
- ½ teaspoon of salt
- ½ cup of dried mushrooms
- 2 cups of lean ground pork.
- 1 stalk celery
- 12 paper wrappers (egg roll)

Directions:
1. Heat a pan over medium heat and add the onion and lean ground pork, cooking for 5 to 7 minutes.
2. Cook for almost 5 minutes with the coleslaw mixture, salt, mushrooms, and celery in the pan.
3. Spread the egg roll wrapper with the contents (1/3 cup), roll it up, and seal with water.
4. Coat the rolls with oil.
5. In an air fryer, cook for 6 to 8 minutes at 400 o F, turning once halfway through.
6. Serve right away.

Nutrition:
- 245 calories
- Fat: 10 g
- Carbohydrates: 9 g.
- Protein content: 11 g

DUMPLINGS WITH PORK

Time to Prepare: 30 minutes
Time to cook: 20 minutes.
4 servings
Ingredients:
- 18 wrappers for dumplings
- 1 tablespoon extra-virgin olive oil
- Bok Choy, 4 cups (chopped)
- Two tbsp rice vinegar
- 1 tbsp. chopped ginger
- 1/4 teaspoon red pepper flakes
- 1 tbsp. minced garlic
- ½ cup of ground lean pork
- Spray cooking oil on
- 2 tsp. light soy sauce
- 1/2 teaspoon of honey
- 1 tablespoon sesame oil, toasted
- 1/8 cup scallions, finely chopped

Directions:
- Preheat the air fryer oven to 400 degrees Fahrenheit (205 degrees Celsius).
- After 6 minutes, add the bok Choy, garlic, and ginger. Place this mixture on a paper towel and pat the excess oil dry.

- In a mixing dish, combine the bok Choy combination, crushed red pepper, and lean ground pork.
- Arrange a dumpling wrapper on a plate and fill with 1 spoonful of filling. Seal and crimp the edges with water.
- Grease the air fryer basket, then add the dumplings and cook for 12 minutes, or until golden.
- In the meanwhile, combine sesame oil, rice vinegar, scallions, soy sauce, and honey in a mixing bowl.
- Toss the dumplings with the sauce.

Nutrition:
- 140 calories
- Fat: 5 g
- 12 grammes of protein
- Carbohydrates: 9 g.

BROCCOLI WITH PORK CHOPS

Time to prepare: 20 minutes.
Time to cook: 10 minutes.
2 servings
Ingredients:
- 2 cups broccoli florets
- Two bone-in pork chops
- paprika, 1/2 teaspoon
- 2 tablespoons of avocado oil.
- 1/2 tablespoon garlic powder
- 1/2 tsp. onion powder
- 2 smashed garlic cloves.
- 1 tsp salt (divided)
- Spray cooking oil on

Directions:
1. Preheat the air fryer to 350 degrees Fahrenheit. Cooking oil should be sprayed on the basket.
2. Combine 1 tablespoon avocado oil, onion powder, 1/2 teaspoons salt, garlic powder, and paprika in a mixing bowl; mix well. Rub this spice mixture over the sides of the pork chops.
3. Place the pork chops in the air fryer basket and cook for 5 minutes.
4. In the meantime, combine 1 teaspoon of avocado oil, garlic, the remaining 1/2 teaspoons of salt, and broccoli in a mixing dish and coat thoroughly.

5. Place the broccoli on top of the pork chop. Cook for another 5 minutes.
6. Take out of the air fryer and serve.

Nutrition:
- 483 calories
- Fat: 20 g
- 12 g carbohydrates
- Protein content: 23 g

CHOPS DE PORK AVEC SAUCE CHEESY

Preparation time: 5 minutes
Time to cook: 4 minutes.
2 servings
Ingredients:
- 4 pork chops (lean)
- 1/2 teaspoon of salt
- 1/2 tablespoon garlic powder
- 4 tablespoons grated cheese
- 2 tablespoons of cilantro, chopped

Directions:
1. Preheat the air fryer to 350 degrees Fahrenheit.
2. Rub the pork chops with garlic, cilantro, and salt.
3. Place the air fryer in the oven. Allow it to cook for 4 minutes.
4. Cook for another 2 minutes on the other side.
5. Sprinkle with cheese and heat for another 2 minutes, or until the cheese is melted.
6. Top with salad greens.

Nutrition:
- 467 calories
- 61 grammes of protein
- Fat: 22 g
- Saturated fat: 8 g

NACHOS WITH PORK RIND

Preparation time: 5 minutes
Time to cook: 5 minutes.
2 servings
Ingredients:

- 2 teaspoons pork rinds
- 1/4 cup shredded cooked chicken
- Half a cup Monterey Jack cheese, shredded
- 1/4 cup sliced pickled jalapeo
- 1/4 cup guacamole
- 1/4 cup sour cream (full fat)

Directions:
1. Arrange pork rinds in a 6-inch circular baking sheet. With grilled chicken and Monterey Jack cheese. Place the pan in the air fryer basket.
2. Preheat the oven to 370 degrees Fahrenheit and set a timer for 5 minutes, or until the cheese is melted.
3. Garnish with jalapeo, guacamole, and sour cream and serve immediately.

Nutrition:
- 295 calories
- Protein content: 30.1 g
- 1.2 grammes of fibre
- 1.8 g carbohydrate
- Fat: 27.5 g
- g carbohydrates

FISH & SEAFOOD RECIPES

AIR FRYER SALMON CAKES

Preparation time: 9 minutes
Time to cook: 7 minutes.
2 servings
Ingredients:
- Fresh salmon fillet (8 oz.)
- 1 egg
- 1/8 salt
- 1/4 tablespoon garlic powder
- 1 sliced lemon

Directions:
1. In a mixing dish, combine the salmon, egg, and seasonings.
2. Make small cakes.
3. Preheat the air fryer to 390 degrees Fahrenheit. Add sliced lemons to the bottom of the air fryer dish; place cakes on top.
4. Bake for 7 minutes. Eat it with your preferred dip according to your dietary needs.

Nutrition:
- 194 calories
- Fat: 9 g
- 1 g carbohydrate
- Protein content: 25 g

SHRIMP IN COCONUT SAUCE

Preparation time: 9 minutes
Time to cook: 8-10 minutes.
4 servings
Ingredients:
- 1/2 cup: 1/2 cup crushed pork rinds
- 4 jumbo shrimp (deveined): 4 giant shrimp
- 1/2 cup of coconut flakes (ideally organic)
- 2 eggs
- 1/2 cup coconut flakes
- 1/2 inch of frying oil of your choice.

- To taste, freshly ground black pepper and kosher salt.

A sauce for dipping:
- As an alternative, 2-3 tbsp powdered sugar
- 3 teaspoons mayonnaise
- 1 gallon soured cream
- 1 tablespoon of coconut essence, or to taste.
- 3 tablespoons of coconut cream.
- To taste, 1/4 teaspoon pineapple flavour
- 3 tablespoons of unsweetened coconut flakes (optional).

Directions:
Sauce:
- Combine all of the dipping sauce ingredients in a small dish (Pineapple flavor). Combine well and chill until ready to serve.

Shrimps:
1. Whisk together all of the eggs in a large mixing bowl and a small shallow mixing dish; stir in the crushed pork rinds, coconut flour, sea salt, coconut flakes, and freshly ground black pepper.
2. Dip the shrimp in the combined eggs, then in the coconut flour mixture, one at a time. Place them on a clean platter or in the basket of your air fryer.
3. Arrange the battered shrimp in a single layer in your air fryer basket.
4. Spritz the shrimp with olive oil and cook for 8 to 10 minutes at 360°F, turning halfway through.
5. Immediately serve with dipping sauce.

Nutrition:
- 340 calories
- Protein content: 25 g
- 9 g carbohydrate
- Fat: 16 g

AIR FRYER CRISPY FISH STICKS

Preparation time: 9 minutes
Time to cook: 10 minutes.
4 servings
Ingredients:
- 1 pound of whitefish (such as cod).
- 1/4 cup of mayonnaise
- 2 tablespoons Dijon mustard

- Two tablespoons water
- 1 ½ cup of rind of pork
- 3/4 teaspoons of Cajun seasoning
- To taste, kosher salt and pepper.
- Spray cooking oil on

Directions:
1. Coat the air fryer rack with nonstick frying spray.
2. After patting the fish dry, cut it into 1 inch by 2 inch sticks.
3. In a small bowl, combine the mayonnaise, mustard, and water. In a separate small container, combine the pork rinds with Cajun spice.
4. Season with kosher salt and freshly ground pepper to taste (both pork rinds and seasoning can have a decent amount of kosher salt, so you can dip a finger to see how salty it is).
5. Working with one piece of fish at a time, dip it in the mayonnaise mixture and tap off the excess. Dip into the pork rind mixture, then turn to cover. Place it on the air fryer rack.
6. Preheat the oven to 400 degrees Fahrenheit for 5 minutes, and then flip the fish with tongs and bake for an additional 5 minutes. Serve

Nutrition:
- 263 calories
- Fat: 16 g
- 1 g carbohydrate
- Protein content: 26.4 g

SALMON WITH HONEY GLAZE

Preparation time: 11 minutes
Time to cook: 16 minutes.
2 servings
Ingredients:
- 6 tablespoons of gluten-free soy sauce
- Salmon fillets, 2 pcs.
- 3 tablespoons of sweet rice wine.
- 1 tablespoon water
- 6 teaspoons of honey

Directions:
1. Combine sweet rice wine, soy sauce, honey, and water in a mixing dish.
2. Set aside half of it.

3. Marinate the fish for 2 hours in half of the sauce.
4. Preheat the air fryer to 180 degrees Celsius.
5. Cook for 8 minutes, turning halfway through, and cook for 5 minute more.
6. After 3 or 4 minutes, baste the salmon with the marinade mixture.
7. Pour half of the marinade into a skillet and reduce to half before serving with a sauce.

Nutrition:
- 254 calories
- Fat: 12 g
- 9.9 g carbohydrates
- Protein (20 g)

SALMON WITH BASIL-PARMESAN CRUST

Preparation time: 5 minutes
Time to cook: 7 minutes.
4 servings
Ingredients:
- 3 tbsp Parmesan cheese, grated
- 4 fillets of skinless salmon.
- a quarter teaspoon of salt
- Black pepper, freshly ground.
- 3 tablespoons of low-fat mayonnaise.
- 1/4 cups of chopped basil leaves
- 1/2 lemon
- Spraying olive oil

Directions:
1. Preheat the air fryer to 400 degrees Fahrenheit. Olive oil should be sprayed on the basket.
1. Season the salmon with salt, pepper, and lemon juice.
2. In a mixing bowl, combine 2 tablespoons Parmesan cheese, mayonnaise, and basil leaves.
3. Top the salmon with this mixture and extra parmesan and cook for 5 minutes.
4. 7 minutes, or until completely cooked.
5. Serve right away.

Nutrition:
- 289 calories
- Fat: 18.5 g, 1.5 g carbohydrates
- Protein 30 g

Cajun Shrimp in the Air Fryer

Preparation time: 9 minutes
Time to cook: 3 minutes.
4 servings
Ingredients:
- 24 extra-jumbo peeled shrimp
- 2 tablespoons of olive oil.
- 1 tbsp. Cajun seasoning
- 1 zucchini, cut into thick slices (half-moons).
- 1/4 cup of cooked turkey
- 2 halved yellow squash
- a quarter teaspoon kosher salt

Directions:
1. In a mixing bowl, combine the shrimp and Cajun spice.
2. Combine zucchini, turkey, salt, and squash in a separate dish and cover with oil. 3.
3. Preheat the air fryer to 400 degrees Fahrenheit.
4. Place the shrimp-vegetable mixture in the fryer basket and cook for 3 minutes.
5. Serve right away.

Nutrition:
- 284 calories
- Fat: 14 g
- 8 g carbohydrate
- Protein: 31 g

Lemon Cod in the Air Fryer

Preparation time: 5 minutes
Time to cook: 10 minutes.
1 serving
Ingredients:
- 1 pound cod fillet
- 1 tablespoon of dried parsley, chopped
- To taste, kosher salt and pepper.
- 1 teaspoon garlic powder
- 1 lemon

Directions:
1. Combine all the ingredients in a dish and coat the fish fillet with spices. 2.
2. Slice the lemon and place it in the air fryer basket.

3. Arrange the seasoned fish on top. Lemon slices should be placed on top of the fish.
4. Cook for 10 minutes at 375°F, or until the salmon reaches an internal temperature of 145°F.
5. Serve

Nutrition:
- 101 calories
- Fat: 1 g
- 10 g carbohydrate
- 16g protein

SALMON FILLETS IN THE AIR FRYER

Preparation time: 5 minutes
Time to cook: 15 minutes.
2 servings
Ingredients:
- 1/4 cup low-fat Greek yoghurt
- 2 fillets of salmon,
- 1 tablespoon chopped fresh dill
- 1 teaspoon lemon juice
- a half teaspoon garlic powder
- Kosher salt with black pepper.

Directions:
1. Slice the lemon and place it in the bottom of the air fryer basket.
2. Season the salmon with freshly ground pepper and kosher salt. Place the salmon on top of the lemons.
3. Bake at 330°F for 15 minutes.
4. Meanwhile, combine the garlic powder, lemon juice, salt, pepper, and yoghurt with the dill.
5. Plate the fish with the sauce.

Nutrition:
- 194 calories
- Fat: 7 g
- 6 g carbohydrate
- Protein content: 25 g

FISH AND CHIPS IN THE AIR FRYER

Preparation time: 11 minutes

Time to cook: 35 minutes.
4 servings
Ingredients:
- 4 cups of any kind of fish fillet
- ¼ cup of all-purpose flour
- 1 cup whole-wheat breadcrumbs
- 1 egg
- 2 tbsp. olive oil
- Two potatoes
- 1 teaspoon sea salt

Directions:
1. Slice the potatoes into fries. Then sprinkle with salt and oil.
2. In an air fryer, cook for 20 minutes at 400°F, tossing halfway through.
3. Meanwhile, coat the fish in flour, then in the whisked egg, and lastly with the breadcrumb mixture.
4. Cook the fish in the air fryer for 15 minutes at 330 °F.
5. If necessary, flip it halfway through.
6. Accompanied with tartar sauce and salad greens,

Nutrition:
- 409 calories
- Fat: 11 g
- Carbohydrates: 44 g.
- Protein 30 g

GRILLED LEMON-GLAZED SALMON

Preparation time: 9 minutes
Time to cook: 8 minutes.
4 servings
Ingredients:
- 2 tablespoons of olive oil.
- 2 fillets of salmon,
- A third cup of lemon juice
- 1/3 cups of water
- 1/3 cup gluten-free light soy sauce
- Honey 1/3 cup
- Topped with scallions
- Black pepper, garlic powder, and kosher salt to taste.

Directions:

1. Season the salmon with salt and pepper.
2. Combine honey, soy sauce, lemon juice, water, and oil in a mixing dish.
3. Marinate the salmon in this marinade for at least 2 hours.
4. Preheat the air fryer to 180 degrees Celsius.
5. Cook the fish for 8 minutes in the air fryer.
6. Arrange on a serving plate and top with scallion slices.

Nutrition:
- 211 calories
- Fat: 9 g, 4.9 g carbohydrate
- Protein: 15 g

NUGGETS OF AIR-FRIED FISH

Preparation time: 15 minutes
Time to cook: 12 minutes.
4 servings
Ingredients:
- 2 cups cubed (skinless) fillets of fish
- 1 egg, beaten
- 5 teaspoons of flour
- 5 teaspoons of water
- To taste, kosher salt and pepper.
- 1/2 cup breadcrumb mix
- 1/4 cup whole-wheat breadcrumbs
- Spray able oil

Directions:
1. Season the fish cubes with freshly ground pepper and kosher salt.
2. In a mixing basin, combine flour and gradually add water, mixing as you go.
3. Finally, fold in the egg. Continue to combine but do not over mix.
4. Dip the cubes into the batter, then into the breadcrumb mixture. Coat thoroughly.
5. Spray the cubes with oil and place them on a baking dish.
6. Preheat the air fryer to 200 degrees Celsius.
7. Cook the cubes in the air fryer for 12 minutes, or until they are thoroughly cooked and golden brown.
8. Garnish with some salad leaves.

Nutrition:
- 184 calories

- Fat: 3 g
- 10 g carbohydrate
- Protein content: 19 g

GRILLED GARLIC ROSEMARY PRAWNS

Preparation time: 5 minutes
11 minutes of cooking time
2 servings
Ingredients:
- 1/2 tbsp. melted butter
- 8 slices of green capsicum
- Eight prawns
- 1/8 cup of rosemary sprigs
- Kosher salt and freshly ground black pepper
- 3-4 garlic cloves, minced

Directions:
1. In a dish, combine all of the ingredients and marinate the prawns for at least 60 minutes.
2. Thread 2 prawns and 2 pieces of capsicum onto each skewer.
3. Preheat the air fryer to 180 degrees Celsius.
4. Continue to cook for 5 to 6 minutes. Cook for an additional 5 minutes after increasing the temperature to 200 o C.
5. Serve with lemon wedges as garnish.

Nutrition:
- 194 calories
- Fat: 10 g
- 12 g carbohydrates
- Protein content: 26 g

VEGETARIAN RECIPES

SURPRISE EGGPLANT

Preparation time: 10-20 minutes
Time to cook: 7 minutes.
4 servings
Ingredients:
- 1 eggplant, roughly sliced
- 3 zucchini, roughly sliced
- three tbsp olive oil (extra virgin)
- 3 tomatoes, sliced
- 2 teaspoons lemon juice
- 1 teaspoon thyme dried
- 1 tsp. dried oregano
- Season with salt and black pepper to taste.

Directions:
1. Place the eggplant slices in the air fryer oven.
2. Add the zucchini and tomatoes and mix well.
3. In a mixing bowl, combine lemon juice, salt, pepper, thyme, oregano, and oil.
4. Pour this over the vegetables, mix to coat, and cook for 7 minutes on high in an air fryer.
5. Quickly remove the pressure, open the top, and divide the contents across plates.

Nutrition:
- 160 calories
- Fat: 7 g
- 1 grammes protein
- 6 g of sugar
- 19 g carbohydrate
- 8 grammes of fibre
- 20 milligrams sodium

Turnips with Carrots

Preparation time: 10-20 minutes
Time to cook: 9 minutes.
4 servings
Ingredients:
- Two peeled and sliced turnips
- 1 sliced small onion
- 1 tsp. lemon juice
- 1 teaspoon ground cumin
- 3 carrots, sliced
- 1 tablespoon of extra-virgin olive oil.
- 1 cup of water
- To taste, season with salt and black pepper.

Directions:
- Heat the oil in your air fryer oven on the "Sauté" setting.
- Cook for 2 minutes after adding the onion.
- Stir in the turnips, carrots, cumin, and lemon juice and simmer for 1 minute.
- Stir in the salt, pepper, and water. Cook for 6 minutes on high with the lid closed.
- Quickly reduce the pressure, remove the air fryer oven cover, and divide the turnips and carrots among plates.

Nutrition:
- 170 calories
- Fat: 9 g
- 1 grammes protein
- 5 g of sugar
- Carbohydrates: 19 g
- 7 grammes of fibre
- 475 milligrams of sodium

In an Instant, Brussels Sprouts with Parmesan

Preparation time: 1020 minutes
Time to cook: 3 minutes.
4 servings
Ingredients:
- 1 pound washed Brussels sprouts
- 1 cup of water
- 3 tablespoons grated Parmesan
- 1 teaspoon lemon juice

- 2 tablespoons of butter.
- Season with salt and black pepper to taste.

Directions:
1. Place sprouts in an air fryer oven and season with salt, pepper, and water. Cook for 3 minutes on high with the lid closed.
2. Release the pressure quickly, transfer the sprouts to a basin, drain the water, and thoroughly clean the pot.
3. Put your pot on "Sauté" mode and melt the butter.
4. Stir in the lemon juice.
5. Stir in the sprouts and transfer to plates.
6. Season to taste with salt and pepper, then top with Parmesan cheese.

Nutrition:
- 230 calories
- Fat: 10 g
- 8 g protein
- 5 g of sugar

FENNEL BRAISED

Preparation time: 1020 minutes
Time to cook: 14 minutes.
4 servings
Ingredients:
- 2 fennel bulbs trimmed and quartered.
- Three tbsp olive oil (extra virgin)
- One-quarter cup white wine
- 1/4 cup grated Parmesan cheese
- 3/4 cup vegetable broth
- Half a cup lemon juice
- 1 garlic clove, sliced
- 1 tablespoon dried red pepper
- To taste, season with salt and black pepper.

Directions:
1. Heat the oil in your air fryer oven on the "Sauté" setting.
2. Add the garlic and red pepper flakes and mix well. Cook for 2 minutes, then remove the garlic.
3. Stir in the fennel and cook for 8 minutes.

4. Season with salt and pepper, and then add the stock and wine, cover, and cook on high for 4 minutes.
5. Quickly release the pressure, open the air fryer oven cover, and add the lemon juice, more salt and pepper, and cheese if desired.
6. Toss to coat, then divide among plates and serve.

Nutrition:
- 230 calories
- Fat: 4 g
- 1 grammes protein
- 3 g of sugar

SALAD WITH BEETS AND ORANGES

Preparation time: 10-20 minutes
Time to cook: 7 minutes.
4 servings
Ingredients:
- Beets weighing 1 1/2 pounds
- 3 strips of orange peel.
- 2 tbsp apple cider vinegar
- Half a cup orange juice
- 2 teaspoon orange zest
- 2 tablespoons of brown sugar.
- Two chopped scallions
- 2 tablespoons mustard
- 2 cups mustard greens and 2 cups arugula

Directions:
1. Scrub the beets well, then cut them in half and place them in a basin.
2. In your air fryer oven, toss together orange peel strips, vinegar, and orange juice.
3. Add the beets, close the air fryer oven cover, and cook for 7 minutes on high before naturally releasing the pressure.
4. Carefully remove the cover and place the beets in a basin.
5. Remove the peel strips from the saucepan; stir in the mustard and sugar until thoroughly combined.
6. Toss the beets with scallions and orange zest.
7. Pour the liquid from the saucepan over the beets, stir to coat, and serve on plates topped with mixed salad greens.

Nutrition:
- 164 calories
- Fat: 5 g
- 2 g of protein
- 5 g of sugar

A Dish with Endives

Preparation time: 10-20 minutes
Time to cook: 7 minutes.
4 servings
Ingredients:
- 4 endives, trimmed
- 2 tablespoons of butter.
- 1 teaspoon of white flour
- 4 ham slices.
- 1/2 teaspoon ground nutmeg
- 14 oz. of milk
- Season with salt and black pepper to taste.

Directions:
1. Place the endives in the steamer basket of your air fryer oven, cover, and cook on high for 10 minutes.
2. Meanwhile, melt the butter in a saucepan over medium heat.
3. Add the flour and cook for 3 minutes.
4. Stir in the milk, salt, pepper, and nutmeg, and then decrease the heat to low and simmer for 10 minutes.
5. Remove the saucepan from the heat, uncover it, and roll each in a piece of ham.
6. Arrange the endives in a pan, pour the milk mixture over them, and place them under a hot broiler for 10 minutes. Slice into slices, place on plates, and serve.

Nutrition:
- 175 calories
- Fat: 8 g
- 1 grammes protein
- 2 g of sugar

ROASTED POTATOES

Preparation time: 10-20 minutes
Time to cook: 17 minutes.
4 servings
Ingredients:
- 2 pound baby potatoes
- 5 tablespoons of vegetable oil.
- 1/2 cup chicken broth
- 1 rosemary sprig
- 5 garlic cloves
- Season with salt and black pepper to taste.

Directions:
1. Heat the oil in your air fryer oven on the "Sauté" setting.
2. Cook for 10 minutes, stirring in the potatoes, rosemary, and garlic.
3. Prick each potato with a knife, and then add the stock, salt, and pepper to the pot, close the air fryer oven cover, and cook for 7 minutes on high.
4. Quickly reduce the pressure, remove the air fryer oven cover, and divide the potatoes among plates.

Nutrition:
- 250 calories
- Fat: 15 g
- 2 g of protein
- Sugar, 1 g

MUSHROOMS STUFFED WITH CHEESE

Timing for preparation: 15 minutes.
7 minutes for cooking.
3 servings
Ingredients
- 9 substantial button mushrooms, stems cut off
- 1-tablespoon of olive oil
- To taste, add salt and black pepper.
- Dried rosemary, 1/2 tsp.
- Shredded Swiss cheese, 6 tablespoons
- Shredded Romano cheese, 6 tablespoons
- 6 teaspoons cream cheese
- Soy sauce, 1 teaspoon
- 1 tsp. minced garlic

- 3 tbsp. minced green onions

Directions:
Olive oil should be used to coat the mushroom caps before adding salt, pepper, and rosemary. Divide the filling mixture among the mushroom caps after carefully combining the other ingredients in a bowl. Cook for 7 minutes at 390°F in a prepared air fryer. Before serving, let the mushrooms gently cool.

Nutrition:
344.5 calories, 27.5g of fat, 10.6g of carbs, 14.8g of protein, and 7.5g of sugar.

SKEWERS WITH MEDITERRANEAN VEGETABLES

Preparation time: 30 minutes
13 minutes for cooking.
4 servings
Ingredients:
- Cut two medium zucchini into 1-inch slices.
- Each of the two red bell peppers, cut into 1 inch chunks
- 1-inch-long slices of a green bell pepper
- Cut one red onion into 1-inch slices.
- Olive oil, two teaspoons
- To taste, sea salt
- 1/2 teaspoon, to taste
- Half the amount of red pepper flakes

Directions:
Veggies are threaded onto skewers; olive oil and spices are then drizzled over the skewers of vegetables. In a preheated air fryer, cook for 13 minutes at 400 degrees F. Serve hot.

Nutrition:
137.6 calories, 9.6 grammes of fat, 9.5 grammes of carbohydrates, 2.8 grammes of protein, and 6.2 grammes of sugars

SNACKS RECIPES

FRIED SWEET POTATOES.

5 minutes for preparation.
Preparation Time: 8 min.
4 servings
Ingredients:
- Peel two medium sweet potatoes.
- 1 tablespoon arrowroot starch
- 2-tablespoon cinnamon
- A quarter cup of coconut sugar
- 2 teaspoons of unsalted melted butter.
- Olive oil, 1/2 tablespoon
- Confectioners make the necessary turns.

Directions:
1. Turn on the air fryer. Place the frying basket inside, lubricate it with olive oil, and then cover it. Then, set the temperature to 370°F and let the fryer heat up for five minutes.
2. In the meantime, slice peeled sweet potatoes into slices that are 1/2 inches thick. Add the oil and starch, stir, and serve.
3. Uncover the fryer, add the sweet potatoes, and cover it with the lid. Cook for 8 minutes, or until the sweet potatoes are pleasantly browned.
4. Upon hearing the air fryer beep, open the cover, remove the sweet potato fries, add the butter, sprinkle the sugar and cinnamon on top, and toss to combine.
5. Top the fries with confectioners' sugar and serve.

Nutrition:
- 130 calories
- 27 g of carbs.
- Fat: 2.3 g, 1.2 g of protein.
- 3 g of fibre.

CHEESE SKEWERS

Preparation time: 5 to 7 minutes
Preparation Time: 5 min.
2 servings
Ingredients:
- 10 spring roll wrappers, divided into quarters.
- 2" x 12" matchsticks of reduced-fat, 1/4 lb. sharp cheddar cheese Spray able oil

Directions:
1. Preheat the air fryer to 400°F.
2. Place the cheese matchstick at the largest end of the quartered spring roll wrapper. Water should be applied to the wrapper's edges and tip.
1. The spring roll wrapper should be folded over the cheese and both ends tucked in.
2. Rolls spring securely all the way to the tip. Put this in a freezer-safe container that has been saran-wrapped. For each cheese and spring roll wrapper, repeat the procedure.
3. Freeze for an hour before frying.
4. Lightly coat the cheese matchsticks with oil. A good-sized handful should be placed in the air fryer basket. Only fry the wrappers for 3 to 5 minutes, or until they are golden brown. Midway through, shake the basket's contents.
5. Take it out of the hamper and put it on. Plates. Repeat the procedure for the remaining breaded cheese sticks. Serve

Nutrition:
- 229 calories
- 16 g of carbs.
- Fat: 10 g
- 15 g of protein. 1.8 g of fibre.

ZOODLES CRISPS

Preparation time: 30 minutes
30 minutes for cooking.
2 servings
Ingredients:
- 2 zucchini, cut into discs that are 1/8 inch thick.
- Sea salt, a pinch
- White pepper, if desired.
- Olive oil, 1 tablespoon, for drizzling

Directions:
1. Set the air fryer's temperature to 330°F.

2. In a mixing bowl, combine the salt and zucchini. Allow it to drain for 30 minutes in a colander.
3. Layer the zucchini in a baking dish. Pour some oil in. Season with pepper. Baked goods should be put in the air fryer basket. For 30 minutes, cook.
4. Season to taste and serve.

Nutrition:
- Calories 15.2,
- -3.6 g of carbs.
- -Fat: 0.1 g,
- -0.6 g of protein.
- -1.3 g of fibre.

Pumpkin Skinny Chips

20 minutes for preparation.
13 minutes for cooking.
2 servings
Ingredients:
- 1 pound of pumpkin, divided into sticks.
- Coconut oil, 1 tablespoon
- 1/2 tablespoon rosemary
- 1/2 tablespoon basil
- To taste, add salt and black pepper.

Directions:
1. Preheat the air fryer to 395 degrees Fahrenheit. Coconut oil should be used to rub the pumpkin sticks before adding the spices and combining.
2. Cook the basket for 13 minutes, shaking halfway through.
3. Add the mayonnaise to the dish. Enjoy!

Nutrition:
- -118 calories
- -Fat; 14.7 g
- -2.2 g of carbs.
- -6.2 g of protein.
- -7 g of sugar.

Ripe Bananas Fried in the Air.

Preparation time: 10 minutes
10 minutes for cooking.
2 servings
Ingredients:
- Two big, ripe plantains peeled and cut into discs one inch thick. Unsweetened coconut butter, 1 tablespoon

Directions:
1. Set the air fryer's temperature to 350°F.
2. Spread a thin layer of coconut butter on the plantain discs.
3. Arrange the ingredients in the air fryer basket in one even layer, avoiding any overlap or contact. For 10 minutes, fry the plantains.
4. Take them out of the hamper. Position on plates. For each plantain, repeat the method.
5. As soon as the plantains are still warm, Serve

Nutrition:
- -209 calories
- -29 g of carbs.
- -Fat: 8 g
- -2.9 g of protein.
- -3.5 g of fibre.

Air-Fried Plantains with Coconut Sauce

10 minutes are required for preparation.
Cooking Time: 10 min.
Servings: 4
Ingredients:
- 6 ripe plantains peeled and quartered lengthwise.
- 1 tin coconut cream
- 2 tablespoons of honey.
- 1 tablespoon of coconut oil.

Directions:
1. Set the air fryer to 330°F.
1. Place a thick-bottomed saucepan over high heat, add the coconut cream, and bring to a boil. Lower the heat to the lowest setting and let the cream simmer uncovered until it has been cut in half and darkened in colour. Turn off the heat.
2. Stir in the honey until smooth. Before use, let it cool fully. Coconut oil should be used to sparingly grease a nonstick pan.

3. Place the plantains in a layer in the air fryer basket and cook for 10 minutes, or until brown on both sides. Drains on paper towels. Place plantains on plates.
4. Add a little bit of coconut sauce. Serve

Nutrition:
- -Calories: 236
- -Carbohydrate content: 0 g
- -Fat: 1.5 g
- -One grammes of protein is
- -1.8 g fibre

BRUSCHETTA WITH BASIL PESTO

Preparation time: 10 minutes
4 to 8 minutes for cooking.
4 servings
Ingredients:
- 8 pieces of 1/2-inch-thick French bread
- 2 tablespoons of softened butter.
- 1 cup shredded mozzarella cheese
- 1/2 cups of pesto with basil
- 1 cup chopped grape tomatoes
- 2 thinly sliced green onions

Directions:
1. Spread the butter on the bread and set it butter-side up in the basket of the air fryer. 2. Bake the bread for 3 to 5 minutes, or until it becomes a light golden brown, at 350 °F (177 °C).
1. Take the bread out of the basket and sprinkle some cheese on top of each slice. Batch-return to the basket and bake for 1 to 3 minutes, or until the cheese is melted.
2. In the meantime, mix the tomatoes, green onions, and pesto in a small bowl.
3. Take the bread out of the air fryer and put it on a serving platter when the cheese has melted. Serve each slice topped with a little of the pesto mixture.

Nutrition:
- 463 calories, Fat: 25 g
- 19 g of protein.
- 41 g of carbs.
- 3 g of fibre.
- 2 g glucose
- Salt: 822 mg.

Apple Cinnamon Chips

Timing for preparation: 15 minutes.
9–13 minutes for cooking.
4 servings
Ingredients:
- Cut two firm Bosc pears crosswise into pieces that are 1/8 inch thick.
- One tablespoon of freshly squeezed lemon juice,
- Ground cinnamon, half a teaspoon.
- 1/8 teaspoon of ground cardamom or nutmeg

Directions:
1. Divide the bigger rounds containing seeds from the smaller stem-end rounds of pears. 2. From the bigger pieces, remove the core and seeds. Add lemon juice, cinnamon, and cardamom to all the slices.
2. Put the smaller chips in the basket. Shake the basket once while air frying at 380 oF (193 oC.) for 3 to 5 minutes, or until light golden brown. From the air fryer, remove it.
3. Repeat with the bigger slices, stirring the basket once throughout the cooking for 6 to 8 minutes, or until light golden brown.
4. Take the tortilla chips out of the oven. Cool before serving, or store at room temperature in an airtight container for up to two days.

Nutrition:
- 31 calories
- Fat: 0 g
- 7 g of protein.
- 8 g of carbs.
- 2 g of fibre.
- Sucrose: 5 g.
- 0 mg NaCl

Triangles of Phyllo vegetables

Timing for preparation: 15 minutes.
6 to 11 minutes for cooking.
2 servings
Ingredients:
- Onion, minced, 3 tbsp.
- 2 minced garlic cloves
- Grated carrot, 2 tablespoons.
- Olive oil, 1 teaspoon
- 3 tbsp frozen baby peas, thawed

- Non-fat cream cheese, 2 tablespoons, at room temperature.
- 6 sheets of thawed frozen phyllo dough.
- To spray olive oil on the dough,

Directions:
1. In a baking dish, combine the onion, garlic, carrot, and olive oil. Vegetables should be air-fried at 390 °F (199 °C) for 2 to 4 minutes, or until crisp-tender. Place it in a basin.
1. Add the cream cheese and peas to the vegetable mixture. While you make the dough, let it cool.
2. Place one phyllo sheet on a work surface and mist with a little olive oil spray. Add one more phyllo sheet on top. You'll have 3 stacks with 2 layers each if you repeat the process with the remaining 4 phyllo sheets. Cut each stack into four strips along the length (12 strips total).
3. Add a little bit of the filling—about 2 teaspoons—to the bottom of each strip. Fold the triangles over like you would a flag: bring one corner up over the filling to form a triangle. Add some water to the edge to seal it. Continue with the remaining filling and strips.
4. Cook the triangles in the air fryer in two batches for 4 to 7 minutes, or until golden brown. Serve

Nutrition:
- 67 calories
- Fat: 2 g
- 2 g of protein.
- 11 g of carbs.
- 1 gramme of fibre
- Sucrose: 1 g.
- 121 mg salt

DESSERTS RECIPES

TAPIOCA PUDDING IS DELICIOUS

Time required for preparation: 10 minutes.
Cooking Time: 8 minutes.
Servings: 4
Ingredients:
- 1/2 cup tapioca pearls
- 1 coconut milk can
- a half-cup liquid
- 4 tbsp. maple syrup.
- 1 quart almond milk
- Pinch cardamom.

Directions:
1. Soak tapioca for one hour in almond milk.
2. In a heat-safe bowl, combine all the ingredients except water and cover with foil.
3. Pour half a cup of water into the air fryer oven, and then set the trivet in the pot.
4. Place the bowl on the trivet.
5. Cover the saucepan with a lid and cook for 8 minutes on manual high pressure.
6. Once complete, let the pressure relaxes normally, and then removes the lid.
7. Combine thoroughly and chill for one hour.
8. Serve with gusto.

Nutrition:
- Calories: 313
- Fat: 18.1 g
- Carbs: 38.4 g.
- 18.5 g sugar
- -2.4 g protein
- 1 milligrams of cholesterol

BREAD PUDDING WITH VANILLA

Time required for preparation: 10 minutes.
Time to cook: 15 minutes
Servings: 4
Ingredients:
- 3 gently beaten eggs.
- 1 tablespoon coconut oil
- 1 teaspoon vanilla
- 4 cup bread cubes
- 1/2 teaspoon cinnamon
- 1/4 cup of raisins
- 1/4 cup of chocolate chips
- 2 quarts milk
- 1/4 tsp. salt.
- 2 gallons of water.

Directions:
1. Pour water into the air fryer's oven, followed by the trivet.
1. Add cubed bread to the baking dish.
2. In a large bowl, combine the rest of the ingredients.
3. Pour the mixture from the bowl over the bread cubes in the baking dish, and then cover the dish with aluminium foil.
4. Position the baking dish on the trivet.
5. Seal the pot with the cover and cook on the steam setting for 15 minutes.
6. Once complete, let the pressure relaxes normally, and then removes the lid.
7. Remove the baking dish from the saucepan with care.
8. Serve with gusto.

Nutrition:
- Calories: 230
- Fat: 10.1 g
- Carbohydrates: 25 g
- Sugar: 16.7 g.
- -9.2 g protein
- Cholesterol: 135 mg

Blueberry Muffins

Time required for preparation: 10 minutes.
Cooking Time: 25 min.
Servings: 4
Ingredients:
- 2 gently beaten eggs.
- 1/4 cup of softened butter
- 1/2 teaspoon baking soda
- 14 tsp. baking powder
- 1 tsp. vanilla extract.
- 12 cup fresh lemon juice
- 1 teaspoon lemon zest
- 1/4 ounce of sour cream.
- a quarter cup milk
- 1 cup of sugar
- 3/4 ounce of ripe blueberries.
- 1 cup regular flour
- 1/4 tsp. salt.
- 1 quart of water

Directions:
1. In a large mixing bowl, combine all of the ingredients and stir well.
2. Fill the air fryer oven with 1 cup of water, then place the trivet inside.
1. Pour batter into the silicone cupcake mould and set it on the trivet.
2. Seal the pot with the cover and cook at high pressure manually for 25 minutes.
5. Once complete, let the pressure relaxes normally, then remove the lid.
3. Serve and enjoy.

Nutrition:
- Calories: 330
- Fat: 11.6 g
- Carbs: 53.6 g.
- Sugar: 36 g.
- -4.9 g protein
- 80 milligrams of cholesterol

MINI CHOCOLATE CAKE

Time required for preparation: 10 minutes.
Cooking Time: 9 minutes.
Servings: 2
Ingredients:
- 2 eggs
- 2 tablespoons swerve
- 1 tablespoon cocoa powder
- 1/2 teaspoon vanilla
- 1 teaspoon baking powder
- 2 tbsp heavy cream
- 1 cup of water
- Cooking spray

Directions:
4. In a container, thoroughly mix all the dry ingredients.
5. Add all the liquid ingredients to the dry ingredients and stir until smooth.
6. Coat two ramekins with cooking spray.
3. Pour 1 cup of water into the air fryer oven and then lay the trivet on top of the saucepan.
4. Pour the batter into the ramekins and set them on the trivet. 6.
7. Cover the pot with its cover and cook at high pressure manually for nine minutes.
8. Once the pressure has been released using the quick-release technique, open the lid.
9. Carefully remove the ramekins from the saucepan and set them aside to cool.
10. Plate and serve.

Nutrition:
- Calories: 143
- Fat: 11.3 g
- Carbs: 15.7 g.
- -7.8 g protein
- 184 milligrams of cholesterol

Flavorful Carrot Halva.

Time required for preparation: 10 minutes.
Cooking Time: 10 min.
Servings: 4
Ingredients:
- 2 cups carrots, shredded
- 2 tablespoons ghee
- 1/2 teaspoon cardamom
- 3 tablespoons of ground cashews.
- a quarter cup of sugar
- 1 quart of milk
- 4 grammes of raw cashews.
- 3 tablespoons raisins

Directions:
1. Pour ghee into the air fryer oven and choose the "Sauté" setting.
1. Add the raisins and cashews to the pan and heat until golden brown.
2. Add the other ingredients, except the cardamom, and mix well.
3. Cover the pot with its cover and cook for ten minutes on manual high pressure.
4. Once complete, let the pressures relax normally, and then remove the lid.
5. Add the cardamom and stir well before serving.

Nutrition:
- Calories: 171
- Fat: 9.3 g
- Carbs: 20.5 g.
- Sugar: 15.2 g.
- -3.3 g protein
- 14 mg (milligrams)

Vermicelli Pudding

Time required for preparation: 10 minutes.
2 minutes of cooking time
Servings: 4
Ingredients:
- 1/3 cup toasted vermicelli
- 6 dates, pitted, sliced
- 3 tbsp cashews, sliced
- 2 tbsp. sliced pistachios
- 1/4 tsp. vanilla

- Saffron, 1/2 teaspoons
- 1/3 cup sugar
- 5 quarts milk
- 3 tablespoons of coconut.
- 2 tablespoons raisins
- 3 grammes almonds
- 2 tablespoons ghee

Directions:
1. Pour ghee into the air fryer oven and choose the "Sauté" setting.
1. Dates, cashews, pistachios, and almonds should be added to the saucepan and cooked for one minute.
2. Add raisins, coconut, and vermicelli to the dish. Stir thoroughly.
3. Add three cups of milk, sugar, and saffron. Blending nicely.
4. Cover the pot with its cover and cook for two minutes on manual high pressure.
5. Once complete, let the pressure relaxes normally, and then removes the lid.
6. Stir in the remaining milk and vanilla extract.
7. Serve with gusto.

Nutrition:
- Calories: 283
- Fat: 13.4 g
- Carbohydrates: 34.9 g
- Sugar: 28.1 g.
- 9 g protein
- 28 mL (milligrams)

CUSTARD WITH YOGURT

Preparation time: 10 minutes
Time to cook: 20 minutes.
4 servings
Ingredients:
- 1 cup yoghurt (unsweetened)
- 1 1/2 teaspoons of ground cardamom
- 1 cup sweetened condensed milk
- 1 gallon milk

Directions:
1. Combine all of the ingredients in a heat-safe bowl. 2.
2. 2. Wrap the bowl with foil.

3. Fill the air fryer oven with 2 glasses of water, and then add the trivet.
4. Place the trivet on top of the basin.
5. Place the lid on the pot and cook on high pressure for 20 minutes.
6. After that, let the pressure drop naturally for 20 minutes before releasing it using the quick-release technique. Remove the lid.
7. Place the custard dish in the refrigerator for 1 hour when it has cooled.
8. Plate the dish and serve.

Nutrition:
- 215 calories
- Fat: 5.8 g
- 33 g carbohydrate
- Sugar content: 32.4 g
- Protein content: 7.7 g
- 23 milligrams of cholesterol

CONCLUSION

Using an air fryer for the first time might be challenging. If you follow the advice in this book, you'll be cooking like a pro in no time! This book has a range of recipes, so you'll never run out of gas while trying to make your favourite cuisine again! Make sure you read the whole book to ensure you understand everything.

There's something to be said for air fryers. When you think about it, they're sort of like a quick lunch without the trouble of cooking. Simply place a piece of bread or your favourite food (or even a sandwich!) in the air fryer oven and let it cook.

Air fryers are useful since they may be used at any time. You may use them to prepare your favourite supper meal or a mid-day snack while you're getting ready. You may also use them to prepare huge meals like breakfast items or ethnic cuisines overnight, saving you time cleaning up after supper.

When utilising an air fryer, though, be cautious about the items you utilise. Some dishes, such as breaded chicken and pancakes with syrup or butter, are difficult or impossible to cook in an air fryer, so avoid using them. There may be other items you wish to avoid as well, so read our article on the Diabetic Air Fryer Cookbook.

The Diabetic Air Fryer Cookbook is a comprehensive guide to getting started with your air fryer. This cookbook is intended to teach you the fundamentals of using an air fryer, enabling you to take advantage of all of its wonderful capabilities. We'll start with a short list of tips and guidelines to help you make sure you're using your air fryer correctly.

The Diabetic Air-Fryer Cookbook offers a wide range of accessories to help you get the most out of your air fryer. We have a lot of tools you can use to fix your air fryer and make sure it works well and lasts as long as possible.

After reading our cookbook, you'll see that we've covered every aspect of using your Diabetic Air Fryer Cookbook. You'll be able to make nutritious cuisine with minimal effort every time and save money in the process! Use this clever and simple-to-use gadget to make healthier choices without sacrificing convenience!

Printed in Great Britain
by Amazon